Praise for
FINDING JESUS, DISCOVERING SELF

By Caren Goldman and William Dols

"An invitation to self-exploration that integrates personal stories, psychological and spiritual insights, poetry and literature. A rich resource for individual readers and groups-for any who seek to understand their own life-journey more fully and deeply." —Marcus Borg, author of *Meeting Jesus Again for the First Time and The Heart of Christianity*

"Goldman and Dols offer a courageous, poetic, and profound understanding of humanity's brokenness and isolation, and our potentials for healing and wholeness." —Amy-Jill Levine, E. Rhodes and Leona B. Carpenter Professor of New Testament Studies, Vanderbilt University Divinity School and Graduate Department of Religion

"William Dols and Caren Goldman highlight key stories in the life of Jesus by drawing upon their own candid autobiographies, skillfully posed questions linked with imaginative exercises, and artfully chosen readings." —Robert Owens Scott, Director of Trinity Institute, and founding editor, *Spirituality And Health* magazine

"Goldman and Dols are spiritual alchemists . . .Their message crosses all religious boundaries. In a world seething with fundamentalist hatred, nothing could be more important." —Larry Dossey, M.D., author of *Healing Beyond the Body, Reinventing Medicine*, and *Healing Words*.

"Powerful nourishment for lives of integrity, faith, and work in our own day." —Edwin M. Yoder Jr., author of *Telling Others What to Think: Recollections of a Pundit*

". . . allows me as a Jewish reader to learn from the life of a great spiritual leader who has been historically off-limits to Jews." —Rabbi Bruce Bromberg Seltzer, Chaplain, Smith College; Religious Advisor, Amherst College; and Director, Smith/Amherst Hillel

"The authors give us the tools we need to explore the archetypal meanings of sacred scripture and to find and embrace the questions that can change our lives." —Margaret Bullitt-Jonas, author of *Holy Hunger* and *Christ's Passion, Our Passions*

"A great study course for a group of open-minded people interested in making sense out of the life of Jesus and out of their own lives." —James Rowe Adams, author of *From Literal to Literary: The Essential Reference Book for Biblical Metaphors*

"A stunning and perceptive book!" —John Shelby Spong, author of *The Sins of Scripture: Exposing the Bible's Texts of Hate to Reveal the God of Love*

"Its combining of the gospel narratives with fearless inquiry, strong confessional voices, and resonant amplifications from poetry, literature, and film speaks to the heart and demonstrates the breadth of the Holy Spirit." —E. H. Rick Jarow, Associate Professor of Religion, Vassar College

"Not only worthwhile reading for our time, but an inspiration for those who choose to walk the path of spiritual awakening and risk living into the questions of Jesus." —Carolyn Craft, Executive Director of WISDOM Radio and host of WISDOM Radio's "Inner WISDOM"

"An ideal companion: clear, compassionate, celebratory, and unique." —Nina Frost, President of The Vocare Group and author of *Soul Mapping*

"An original approach to the quest for the figure of Jesus that invites its readers to enter the quest not only to seek Jesus but to discover themselves in a process that brings together the eternal and the experiential." —William R. Herzog II, Sallie Knowles Crozer Professor of New Testament Interpretation, Colgate Rochester Crozer Divinity School

"An autobiographical exegesis that is capable of transforming those who participate in it. I could scarcely put it down." —Dr. Walter Wink, Professor of Biblical Interpretation, Auburn Theological Seminary

"This book offers a wealth of reflections and penetrating questions to last a lifetime." -Rev. D. Andrew Kille, PhD, Director of Interfaith Space and author of *Psychological Biblical Criticism*

"A deep well of refreshing water for the seeker, the believer, the preacher and the person in the pew." —The Very Rev. Tracey Lind, Dean of Trinity Cathedral, Cleveland, and author of *Interrupted by God: Glimpses from the Edge*

". . . gives the reader permission to stop longer than a moment, to imagine treasures buried around us and within us, to explore intriguing thoughts that once flew by, and to gain a breathless perspective for living a full life." —The Rt. Rev. William E. Swing, Episcopal Bishop of California

"If you read this book once, as you should, it will find a permanent place on your bookshelf... a religious treasure trove, filled with memorable quotations that go deep . . ." —The Rev. Earl K. Holt III, Minister, King's Chapel, Boston

"Whether you're trying to find your voice, licking your wounds, or just trying to make the next decision about how to live your life, this is the book to help you live into that likeness." —Ana Hernandez, author of *The Sacred Art of Chant*

"An invaluable resource to those of us working in multi-faith contexts." —Jennifer L. Walters, Dean of Religious Life, Smith College

"Blend together the Wisdom of Jesus, the psychological insights of Carl Jung, the integration of Elizabeth Boyden Howes, and the lively experience of the authors and the results are the book in your hands." —John Beverley Butcher, author of *The Tao of Jesus* and *Telling the Untold Stories*

CAREN GOLDMAN and TED VOORHEES

Across the Threshold, Into the Questions

discovering Jesus, finding self

MOREHOUSE PUBLISHING

Unless otherwise noted, the Scripture quotations contained herein are from the New Revised Standard Version Bible, copyright (c) 1989 by the Division of Christian Education of the National Council of Churches of Christ in the U.S.A. Used by permission. All rights reserved.

Morehouse Publishing, 4775 Linglestown Road, Harrisburg, PA 17112

Morehouse Publishing, 445 Fifth Avenue, New York, NY 10016

Morehouse Publishing is an imprint of Church Publishing Incorporated.

Cover art by Jane E. Voorhees

Cover design by Corey Kent

Library of Congress Cataloging-in-Publication Data

Goldman, Caren.
    Across the threshold, into the questions : discovering Jesus, finding self / Caren Goldman and Ted Voorhees.
       p.   cm.
    Includes bibliographical references (p.) and index.
    ISBN 978-0-8192-2255-8 (pbk.)
    1. Bible. N.T. Gospels—Meditations. I. Voorhees, Ted. II. Title.
BS2555.54.G65   2008
232—dc22

2008024178

Printed in the United States of America

08   09   10   11   12   13   10 9 8 7 6 5 4 3 2 1

CONTENTS

To Bill Dols
for blessing our journeys,
spirits, and questions, and

for all that has been and will be
in ways that words cannot express.

ABOUT THE AUTHORS

Caren Goldman, a Jewish author and award-winning journalist, specializes in writing about spirituality, psychology, health, religion, and the arts and humanities. She is the author of *Healing Words for the Body, Mind, and Spirit: 101 Words to Inspire and Affirm* (Marlowe & Co.), the co-author of *Finding Jesus, Discovering Self: Passages to Healing and Wholeness* (Morehouse Publishing), and the writer of *Vitality and Wellness: An Omega Institute Mind, Body, Spirit Book* (Dell), a regular contributor and former senior editor of *The Bible Workbench*, and a former assistant editor of the *Cleveland Jewish News*. For over thirty years, hundreds of her freelance articles about the intersections of spirituality, health, and religion have appeared in national magazines as well as major metropolitan daily and weekly newspapers. Caren began her writing career as a news and features reporter at the *Cleveland Plain Dealer*. She also leads seminars and retreats throughout the country and works as a Bridgebuilder™ conflict resolution consultant to congregations and nonprofit organizations. Caren also plays an accordion to amaze and amuse—mostly herself. She and her husband, Ted Voorhees, live in Florida and North Carolina. Caren can be contacted by e-mail at wordsforhealing@aol.com or via her website: www.carengoldman.com.

Edwin "Ted" Voorhees is an Episcopal priest who has served congregations in North Carolina, Virginia, Ohio, and Massachusetts. He has written for Forward Day-By-Day and is an associate editor of and regular contributor to *The Bible Workbench*. Ted is also a popular retreat, seminar, and workshop leader. As a Bridgebuilder™ conflict resolution consultant and a

Healthy Congregations™ facilitator, he works with congregations in many denominations as well as with non-profit organizations. Presently living in the St. Augustine area of northern Florida and Asheville, North Carolina, he enjoys playing golf with his wife, Caren Goldman, and listening to her accordion concerts. Ted can be reached by e-mail at BerkanaTed@aol.com.

ACKNOWLEDGMENTS

The word acknowledgments fails to express the gratitude we have for the contributions the people below made to *Across the Threshold, Into the Questions: Discovering Jesus, Finding Self.* As we set out to write this book, our plate overflowed with all the things that happen, as the cliché reminds us, "when you are making other plans." This included many of the events and losses that became snapshots of our lives in the Reflections section in each chapter. Among them, a transition toward retirement from a life-long career, a journey to live in another state, and the adventure of discovering what was on the other side of the threshold we crossed as we left the north behind for new life in the south. There was also the declining health of our last surviving parent and her death, the sale of our beloved "vacation" home and retreat center in yet another state, some minor health issues, and spirits that begged to live into grief while smiling at the prospects of new life. Through all the phone calls, e-mails, rationalizations, and justifications about the impact of those events on our writing schedule, Nancy Fitzgerald, our editor, never lost "faith" in our ability to finish in a timely manner and make the second book in this series be all that it could be. Appreciation for her guidance, kind words, and editing that often helped to save us from ourselves, comes from deep within our hearts and souls.

Amy-Jill Levine, the E. Rhodes and Leona B. Carpenter Professor of New Testament Studies at Vanderbilt Divinity School and self-described "Yankee Jewish feminist," honored and also blessed our journey with her interest in *Across the Threshold* and commitment to write the foreword. Her eagle-eye ability to see words or phrases in ways that either a Christian or a Jew might misinterpret them as well as her willingness to be in discussion about each chapter was a gift that kept giving. Indeed, that gift continues to give each time we discuss and debate the meaning of a gospel passage for the first time or the hundredth.

And finally, we want to express heartfelt thanks to all those whose teaching, mentoring, parenting, companionship, stories, eyes, ears, and experiences help us to remember, daily, that there will always be a cost and promise to opening new doors or reopening old ones, crossing those thresholds, learning from the past, living challenging questions, and being choicemakers on roads not taken and those taken again as though for the first time.

FOREWORD

The Gospels serve for many as a source of instructions and assurances: believe this, do that, and inherit eternal life. But these texts are also fonts of challenges and questions: can we imagine a different world that follows divine rather than human standards? Can we chart a course for the future informed but not constrained by the past? Instead of focusing on "eternal life," as did the obnoxious lawyer whose story begins the famous "Parable of the Good Samaritan," can we find the means to live now, with life abundant?

To ask questions of the Gospels or, better, to recognize the questions they pose, neither contradicts traditional Christian belief in the divinity of Jesus nor compromises the beliefs of non-Christians. Caren Goldman and Ted Voorhees—one a Jew and the other a Christian—approach the Gospels at the place where Jews and Christians and indeed people of any or even no religious affiliation can meet: the story of Jesus of Nazareth, a story of a fully human first-century Jew.

Ted and Caren do not sacrifice their personal beliefs on the altar of interfaith sensitivity; nor do they simplistically map twenty-first century perspectives onto the time of the Gospels, as if two thousand years in a second can be erased. The personal connections they make to the story of Jesus are appropriately allusive and elusive, even as both historical understanding and literary sensitivity inform them. The meanings they find, and those they encourage their readers to find, emerge in the encounter between stories told across time and space and culture.

It is in this encounter that new answers can be found to the questions the gospels pose and that we are still asking: who do people say that we are, and who do we claim ourselves to be? Why do we fail to embrace our vulnerability even as we fail to recognize our strengths? How do we face sickness and death, violence and bigotry, poverty and alienation? Where are vocations to be found, thresholds to be crossed, and sacred moments to be encountered? What divides us, and what prompts reconciliation? When is the time to resist or reflect; when should we, or must we, act or react or remain silent? Enriching the possible answers, this volume offers citations from poets and prophets, politicians and pundits, so that the conversation becomes global. The dances among voices take graceful steps to ever-new meaning.

Encountering the gospel stories and juxtaposing them to our own—for our own stories too are sacred—creates instruction and challenge, assurance and question. In the meeting, the strange becomes familiar, the familiar is seen in new ways: reassessment and revision lead to greater clarity, and, inevitably and blessedly, to new possibilities for wholeness. Hearing the stories of Jesus and telling our own does not erase the problems, the doubts, and the fears that mark our lives, but engaging the questions the stories prompt provides us the courage to live and the vision to find the Kingdom of Heaven among us (Luke 21:17).

—Amy-Jill Levine
E. Rhodes and Leona B. Carpenter
Professor of New Testament Studies,
Vanderbilt University Divinity School and
Graduate Department of Religion

INTRODUCTION

About six months after Caren's book *Finding Jesus, Discovering Self: Passages to Healing and Wholeness* appeared in bookstores, we traveled to Boston for her to speak at an ecumenical luncheon sponsored by the Massachusetts Bible Society. Of the many questions asked, two were inevitable.

"You're Jewish. So why are you writing about Jesus?" said an elderly woman who mentioned she was an Episcopalian. "And," she added, "do you believe in him?"

Before answering, Caren mentioned that the woman's questions were precisely the ones that people in Ted's church and in her synagogue asked her when they first heard she was writing *Finding Jesus, Discovering Self*. Now, after months of struggling with variations on a response that would make sense to those who called a Jewish man from Nazareth "Christ" and to Jews who often referred to Jesus as *"that* man," she replied:

"I write about Jesus because he was Jewish and few Jews write about him or understand him historically. He was never a Christian and neither (despite the reasoning of those apt to argue otherwise) was his mother. He was born a Jew, he lived his life as a Jew, and he died a Jew. As for whether or not I believe in Jesus—when asked the same question, Martin Buber, the great Jewish philosopher, scholar, and writer, reportedly answered, 'I believe *with* him.' As someone who was not only born a Jew but attends synagogue and practices Judaism, so do I."

So does Ted, who during thirty-plus years of ordained ministry has spent over 1,500 Sundays challenging Christian worshippers and doubters in

Episcopal pews in North Carolina, Virginia, Ohio, Massachusetts, and Florida to set preconceived notions about the chapters and verses in the Gospels aside in order to make room to hear and see those ancient words anew:

"Why," he asks, "might the Gospel of Mark say that the Holy Spirit immediately *drove* Jesus into the wilderness after his baptism, but Luke and Matthew report that the Spirit *led* him?"

"When Jesus says, 'Your sins are forgiven,' what does he say—or *not* say—about himself?"

"What might it mean for each of you to take seriously what Jesus took seriously?"

In this book, we invite Jews, Christians, people of all faiths, and people who claim no religious or spiritual paths whatsoever to unpack, in their own way and at their own pace, questions about a historical Jew from Nazareth of Galilee. Questions about Jesus that may never have cropped up, been considered, or even cared about before. And questions that may have been tucked away until they could, at last, leap out of the text, leave hiding places between the lines, and give voice to their demands for attention. Indeed, as in *Finding Jesus, Discovering Self*, what we will not do is offer opinionated, theological, or greeting card depictions and analyses of Jesus. Instead, our goal will be to act as midwives who can assist you in your innate ability to birth and nurture your own questions, reflections, and even doubts about the life, journey, meaning, and importance of this first-century Jewish man. We imagine these will be probing and probably puzzling questions that will invite or compel you to re-examine long-held beliefs, continue the journey, take stands, and see the worlds around you—and the worlds within your psyche and soul—with the curious eyes of an explorer willing to enter doorways, cross thresholds, and navigate terra incognita.

Night is Nobel laureate Elie Wiesel's terrifying autobiographical account of the Nazi death camps. The slim volume opens with his description of a fortuitous encounter with a poor, humble, and awkward Hasidic Jew named Moishe the Beadle.

In 1941 both Wiesel, 11, and Moishe the Beadle lived in the Transylvanian town of Sighet. The Nazis had not yet displaced the community, and Wiesel, a devout Jew who believed "profoundly," had asked his father if he could study Kabbalah with a master. His father replied that the great sage Maimonides had said, "One must be thirty before venturing into the world of mysticism, a world fraught with peril. First you must study the basic subjects, those you are able to comprehend. . . There are no Kabbalists in Sighet."

Refusing to be discouraged or dissuaded by either Maimonides or a stubborn parent, Wiesel found his own master one evening when Moishe the Beadle approached him and asked why he wept as he prayed. Thrown off guard and troubled by the "strange question," Wiesel replied that he didn't know why because he had never asked himself that question:

> I cried because . . . because something inside me felt the need to cry. That was all I knew.
>
> "Why do you pray?" he asked after a moment.
>
> Why did I pray? Strange question. Why did I live? Why did I breathe?
>
> "I don't know," I told him, even more troubled and ill at ease. "I don't know."
>
> From that day on, I saw him often. He explained to me, with great emphasis, that every question possessed a power that was lost in the answer. . . .
>
> Man comes to God through the questions he asks Him, he liked to say. Therein lies the true dialogue. Man asks and God replies. But we don't understand his replies. We cannot understand them. Because they dwell in the depths of our souls and remain there until we die. The real answers, Eliezer, you will find only within yourself.
>
> "And why do you pray, Moishe?" I asked him.
>
> "I pray to the God within me for the strength to ask Him the real questions." They spoke that way almost every evening and remained in the empty synagogue, sitting in the semi-darkness where only a few half-burnt candles provided a flickering light.
>
> One evening Wiesel told him how unhappy he was not to be able to find a master to teach him the Zohar, the Kabbalistic works, the secrets of Jewish mysticism. Moishe the Beadle smiled indulgently and after a long silence he said,
>
> "There are a thousand and one gates allowing entry into the orchard of mystical truth. Every human being has his own gate. He must not err and wish to enter the orchard through a gate other than his own. That would present a danger not only for the one entering but also for those who are already inside."
>
> And Moishe the Beadle, the poorest of the poor of Sighet, spoke to me for hours on end about the Kabbalah's revelations and its mysteries. Thus began my initiation. Together we would read, over and over again, the same page of the Zohar. Not to learn it by heart but to discover within the very essence of divinity.
>
> And in the course of those evenings I became convinced that Moishe the Beadle would help me enter eternity, into that time when question and answer would become ONE.[1]

Nigerian author and poet Ben Okri speaks of three kinds of stories: stories we live, stories we tell, and stories "that help our souls fly up towards the greater light." Page after page, you will discover that embedded in the heart of this book are Gospel stories that for nearly two thousand years have been told, lived daily, and engaged to empower souls to open and soar through long-locked doorways and well beyond. And whether or not you are one who has grown up hearing, reading, or praying about the events reported in the Gospels, all of the stories they tell raise two overarching questions that beg consideration: first, what might these stories about Jesus' life, teachings, and death two thousand years ago really say about what he took seriously in his lifetime? And what might they have the power to teach us today—word-by-word, passage-by-passage, and story-by-story about our choices to grow up, take responsibility for the face staring at us in the mirror, and, ultimately, become our own gatekeepers within the orchards of mystical truth?

Contrary to conventional wisdom, careful readings of the Gospels leave little doubt as to Jesus' abiding commitment to his religious roots and to the words, teachings, and commandments in the Torah. At times, those stories report that in his ever-deepening relationship to the Divine, he pondered and questioned the intent and meaning of being a choicemaker concerning certain "Thou shalts" and "Thou shalt nots." However, nowhere do these texts suggest, state, or scream that he abandoned the laws set forth in the Torah or that he ever told others to do the same. Whether in the wilderness, in towns throughout Galilee, in a synagogue, in the Temple in Jerusalem, and even, it is recorded, in those moments before he died, those who told and retold stories about Jesus rooted him and his words deeply in the history, lore, and law of his ancestors.

So what might it mean to live questions—your questions—in order to mine the Gospels for clues and insights about what those stories may have said to audiences two thousand years ago? Moreover, what might they also say to us today about our outer world(s), our inner world, and our own unique relationship to the Divine?

In this book we bid you to close familiar doors behind you and embark on an open-ended journey to find, in your own way, your own answers to those questions. To read the texts with curious, unfiltered eyes to discover information about this first-century Jew that you may not have considered, reconsidered, or uncovered before. We also request that you allow your own estimates and guesstimates about who Jesus might have been to surface through a personal experience of reading the text that acknowledges your own perspective. In so doing, it is our hope that the following records of the life of Jesus as reported in the Gospels, as well as his actions, questions, and doubts, will serve as magnifying glasses that can help you discover and recover lost parts and missing pieces of your psyche and soul that yearn for expression, understanding, and acknowledgement.

Often, challenges to undertake inquisitive journeys into biblical texts without a lifetime of parental, clerical, theological, and scholarly guideposts to map them out can be intimidating and, perhaps, frightening. Where, when, and how do I begin to trust my process, my fleeting thoughts, my doubts, and my conclusions? Who are the voices in my head that speak to me, challenge me, and occasionally wag a finger while lecturing me about my new understandings, insights, and revisions to my worldview? Is one of them my voice? Or another's from the past or the present? Or a still small voice within that has patiently waited to speak its truth?

Annie Dillard speaks of the challenges that must be overcome during journeys to mine one's psyche and soul for such undisclosed ruminations, beliefs, questions, and treasures in her book *Teaching a Stone to Talk*.

> *In the deeps are the violence and terror which psychology has warned us. But if you ride these monsters deeper down, if you drop with them farther over the world's rim, you find what our sciences cannot locate or name, the substrate, the ocean or matrix or ether which buoys the rest, which gives goodness its power for good and evil its power for evil, the unified field: our complex and inexplicable caring for each other, and for our life together here. This is given. It is not learned* [2]

For most of us, new journeys through doorways leading to paths and places farther over rims geographical and psychological always begin with questions beckoning us to take the first step over a threshold. Questions that pester, please, probe, frustrate, excite, disturb, enlighten, invite, frighten, as well as absurd questions and incomplete questions that come alive, birth answers that birth new questions, and, with proper nurture, take on a life of their own. Questions that arrest our attention—sometimes for a second, more often for a lifetime—may include:

- How might my religious, secular, and psychic roots and worldviews filter and color the ways I choose to live my life?
- What do I yearn to see, touch, understand, be, and become before I die?
- Am I courageous enough and individual enough to risk venturing beyond the established boundaries of my inner and outer worlds to satisfy those yearnings?
- What might have to change in order for me to be a more confident choicemaker?

- Do I have a voice strong enough to challenge and speak truth to the powers around me and within me?
- Do I, _____, know what I am willing to die for—today, here, now?

In *The Book of Lights* by Chaim Potok, Gershon Loran is a young rabbinical student who must serve a Jewish chaplaincy in Korea during the Cold War. Flashbacks take us to the young rabbi's ongoing struggles to face the dark realities of his inner and outer worlds and discern his future. Will he follow the traditional path of most rabbis and Jewish scholars before him and immerse himself in studies of the Talmud and other writings bearing stamps of institutional approval? Or will he follow his non-conventional seminary mentor into the depths of Kabbalah?

One night, far from familiar groundings in New York or from oft-traveled wastelands in Korea, Gershon awakens in a hotel room in Tokyo and finds himself in a persistent tension.

> This was the hour he had learned to dread, the hour of questions. No time of day or night seemed so filled with the weight of darkness as this hour before the twilight of morning when there hovered about him what he had come to call the four-o'clock-in-the-morning questions.
>
> Listen, listen came the seductive whisper from the darkness. I journey from the other side with a burden of chill truths. Why are you so afraid? Is it possible that illusion is more welcome to you than truth? Listen. Listen.

Lying in the darkness, Gershon listens, silently, to the messenger's litany of comments, admonishments, and questions—pressing, unshakable, burdensome observations and queries that pressure him to go deeper into shadow worlds.

> I ask cruel questions of truth, Gershon. Truth. I come from the other side.
>
> How cold it was now in the room, how dark. The dimmest of lights seemed to have been drained from the air. Was this the realm of the other side? Yet there were truths in those words. How could truths emanate from such darkness? His heart thudded wildly. He lay silent, wondering.

Time passes and the voice breaking through the silence asks: *"Is it that you are surprised at the energies and insights possessed by the realm of darkness?"* The voice then continues, filling the room with more "truths" until a faint stirring in the darkness and a sigh signal the visit is over.

> I leave now. It is almost light. Your illusions will soon return. Ponder my questions. I do not make the journey from the other side merely to torment you. We can make a cautious alliance, you and I. You have a mystic sense,

and an eagerness to break old barriers and confront the new. Old ascents bore you. Am I not right, Gershon? In truth, we are all you have left if you wish to attempt new answers. Leave the dust to the pious and the old, to the professional peddlers of illusions. Shall we not deal in truths? Ah, I feel the light below the rim of your world. What contempt you will have for me soon! Now you still have in you the respect of fear. But soon— Consider. There is some merit in darkness. There are times when light is a menacing distraction. You need the fires of the other side, dear Gershon, if you are to move beyond the pale of the old and the dry and the illusions that are truly dust.[3]

Be it yesterday or today, questions that taunt, test, and tempt us to go to the rim instead of other places often show up at inconvenient times. When approached by such questions and find they point to the positive sides of our hope for a better life now and our imagined landscape of eternal life, our nature is to stay calm, cool, open-hearted, and open-minded, and maybe act curious about them with a smile. However, when unsolicited questions flaunt darkness, the death of a familiar way of life, and offer little or no hope of something new, we tend to behave defensively. Instead of responding from that open, welcoming, and inquisitive place within, we react by either fighting the realities the uncomfortable and painful questions may reveal or by fleeing far from the rim to familiar places where we can safely pretend that they don't exist.

However, no matter where we go, there we are, only to find, as Gershon did, that questions concerning our chill truths that may be caught in the tension between dark and light and between good and evil linger and wait for us beyond the pale of old and dry illusions. Such are the tensions that Jesus encountered when faced with Satan's tests in the wilderness—tests, trials, and temptations that Jesus chose not to resist, but to face and then respond to with an authority rooted in his Jewish upbringing and traditions.

For nearly two thousand years, images of Jesus the Jew as a potential choicemaker have been disguised, discounted, hidden, and even buried by stained-glass institutions, ivory towers, countless clergy, and the media. In turn, ideas that Jesus' inner authority might be the product of mature thinking and personal choices have been dismissed and considered unlikely, if not absurd, by those who believe that the decision to go to Jerusalem was never his to make. If that belief is the foundation of your faith, we ask that you not abandon it, but try experimenting with this book as a way to look through a different lens to view these Gospel stories from another perspective. Rabbi Israel ben Eliezer, who was known as the Baal-Shem, said, "Every man should behave according to his 'rung.' If he does not, if he seizes the 'rung' of a fellow-man and abandons his own, he will actualize neither the one nor the other." Said another way, the goal is to know yourself and take responsibility for giving yourself permission—to authorize yourself—to claim your worldview and see Jesus with your own eyes. The right to your own opinions and conclusions about Jesus is yours and with it the knowledge that you can change your mind at any time.

Among Jews, the phrase "two Jews, three opinions" is not just a saying. Within Jewish communities, multiple opinions are cherished rather than discouraged. The fact that one can question, debate, and discuss one's understanding of God with others (and still go to lunch afterward) is ingrained in the psyche, soul, and, perhaps, the DNA of religious and secular Jews alike. And, according to all the canonical Gospel accounts, Jesus, a human Jew from Nazareth of Galilee on a journey from Nazareth to Jerusalem, was no different.

Within each of us is one who instinctively knows that no matter how strange, frightening, or chilling the truths in our "four-o'clock-in-the-morning questions" may be, they contain calls to be still and silent. Indeed, whether we are in our beds at twilight, driving to the office, dining with friends, lovers, kids, co-workers, or relatives, or gazing at our faces in the bathroom mirror or our navels below, the voice that beckons from the rim can rarely be given voice any other way. In his startling poem, *Sometimes*, the poet David Whyte tells us that the intent of such questions is to make requests that stop us from what we're doing right now and stop what we're becoming while we're doing it.

Sometime shortly before or after the first century CE, Jesus, the Jew from Nazareth, stopped what he was doing and becoming and left everything familiar for wildernesses. By example, the Gospel stories, questions, reflections, quotations, poetry, and prose in this book may, indeed, take you to some wilderness of your own. And by example, for us to take seriously what Jesus took seriously in the accounts we have of his human journey, we, too, must be willing to stop what we're doing and stop what we're becoming and listen to potentially life-changing questions and voices. To stop and unlock, throw open doors, step over thresholds, and continue onward. To find the rims in our psychic and outer worlds. And to let go. To let go, as Jesus did when he left Nazareth.

SUGGESTIONS FOR USING THIS BOOK

The first book in this series, *Finding Jesus, Discovering Self: Passages To Healing And Wholeness*, explores many of the Gospel stories about Jesus' journey from Nazareth of Galilee in a linear way. The opening chapters follow his departure from his hometown, his baptism, and his experiences in the wilderness. The book ends with his arrival in Jerusalem. As he journeys across the pastoral countryside where he grew up and into the cosmopolitan heart of his religious, social, and political beliefs, readers encounter familiar characters. Among them are those who challenge Jesus as teacher, healer, leader, and first-century Jew, those who are taught, healed, and led in his presence, and one who betrays him.

Although *Across the Threshold, Into the Questions: Discovering Jesus, Finding Self* is a companion volume, you do not have to go back to the first one to explore the literal, psychic, and metaphorical terrain of these Gospel stories. Moreover, because this book is not based in part on a timeline, if your perusal of the contents seems to shout, "Start here," and that means chapter 4 or 12—do it.

As always, our goal is to invite and encourage you to *live* this book's questions about the life, teachings, questions, and doubts of Jesus:

- by realizing that the Gospels differ in the language and scenarios they use to tell many of the same stories about Jesus.
- by putting explanations about the text from parents, clergy, professors, and others and your preconceived notions about what it says on a shelf for a while. And since it is your shelf, you can always take what you need or want from it at any time.

- by recalling that in the records of Jesus' life he is a first-century Jewish man known as Jesus of Nazareth. As he wandered throughout Galilee, Jesus worshiped in a synagogue and did not go to or found a church.
- by being open to the many ways in which possibility and mystery knock on our doors with requests to enter our lives.
- by remaining in the center of opposing forces past and present, living and dead, that tug your mind, heart, and even your soul toward conventional answers.
- by staying with and allowing any tensions you may experience to have a voice that can stimulate new thoughts, insights, and feelings about the text, the questions, and your predetermined conclusions about them.
- by knowing that you may never have answers or *the* answer to the questions raised for you in this book.
- by accepting that you can always change your mind about your understanding of what is written and implied between the lines of the text about Jesus, his world, the wide world around you, and the known and unknown worlds within.

In other words, the best way to begin reading, pondering, and living the questions throughout *Across the Threshold* is to see it as a process and be assured that there are no "right" or "wrong" ways to do that. Approach the Gospel texts, the personal Reflections, the questions in Wonderings and Wanderings, and the quotations, poetry, fiction, and nonfiction in Mirrors with a spirit of openness. Of course we would suggest you start each chapter by reading the Gospel text to get centered on a theme. View and review it through different lenses: as a historical account, as a story, as a mythic truth, and as a guidepost pointing you to doorways that separate "what is" within familiar spaces from "what can be" on the other side of the thresholds. Additionally, if you begin working with a set of questions and find yourself more intrigued by new ones that come to mind, write them down and use the process in this book to allow them to guide you to new places and discoveries. The same is true of the additional readings. If one makes you think of another that's not in the book, revisit what those lines of poetry and prose may be saying to you.

We designed the exercises to help you experience the stories about Jesus holistically—not just in your head, but in your body, psyche, and soul, too. Throughout the years that we have led retreats and workshops nationwide, the attendees' responses to experiential exercises taught us that *Finding Jesus* readers who use visualization, music, art materials, mime, and movement to help awaken other senses and ways of knowing the texts will enjoy diving into those waters in this book.

However, we realize for some of you just the idea of doing them may be daunting. You are not alone. Reasons for rejecting the invitation range from disinterest to feeling awkward, self-conscious, and even fearful. Reactions such as those are usually justified. When asked why he has never chanted an entire service, Ted will habitually roll his eyes and then tell a story about his first Sunday as the new priest in a congregation in Virginia. Traditionally, the opening hymn in mainline churches is a call for God's Spirit to enter and be in the midst of the people during the service. When the hymn began that Sunday, Ted sang loudly and proudly as he processed behind the acolytes and choir from the back of the sanctuary to the chancel. After the service ended, a choir member pulled him aside. "That was embarrassing. Didn't anyone ever tell you that you can't sing—that you're practically tone deaf?" He waited for her to crack a smile or say something else. She didn't. Not until he left that congregation's pulpit for another did he once again begin quietly singing the hymns instead of silently mouthing the words. For many of us, when a disapproving voice of authority uttered *cannot*, *should not*, and *must not*, a dimension of our souls took flight. Today, those words can still prevent that stifled and remote part of our spirits from returning to help us express our innate creative abilities. If you find yourself among those saying, "Not me. Not now," take a deep breath and ask: "Where does my resistance come from? Who or what told me I could not or should not draw, sing, write, or move to music—the music on my stereo or iPod, the music of falling water, or the music of my own piper or drummer?" Then, if you decide to go further, taste test our recipes below for using the book and remember—add your own ingredients to help make them familiar, special, and yours forever:

- Give yourself permission to do what feels comfortable and let the rest go. You can always return to the other activities and suggestions later.
- Play soft, slow music without lyrics, such as Pachelbel's Canon in D, Bach's Air on a G String, and similar pieces by Mozart, other classical composers, and your favorite contemporary recording artists.
- Remember that none of the exercises in this book asks you to draw a picture. Instead, several suggest that you "express" your thoughts, feelings, and responses to parts of a story by using art materials. If that means just putting a pencil line or a scribble on a piece of paper

or using chalk to do the same on a sidewalk, give it a try. If using other media to make two- or three-dimensional objects and collages works for you, then keep those "tools" close by. Think crayons, markers, watercolors, clay, old magazines, a camera, and whatever else appeals and feels user friendly.

- The bibliography will point you in the direction of new scholarship about Jesus and his times. It also lists related contemporary writings about the intersections of mind, body, and spirit.

- Finally, to help you explore the biblical texts imaginatively, we include a list of films portraying the life of Jesus on the big screen and television. For the most part, these are not NBC, Arts & Entertainment, History Channel or independent documentary films that search for the historical Jesus or use the exact words of The King James Bible or another translation of a gospel to re-enact the story. Instead, they are creative, filtered, and interpretive attempts to show Jesus' life from a director's personal point of view. Controversy and even media frenzies have surrounded one or more of these films. All have left a cinematic imprint on the ways in which Gospel stories can be experienced and retold. No matter how your unique view of Jesus' life informs your beliefs about him, try to view one or more of these films through a wide lens. Take note of your responses and reactions to what you see and feel and wonder how the story in movies for the masses may have "reel" value for you. Indeed, while not necessarily true or factual, one or more may generate new insights, points of view, questions, and even truths about Jesus, his life and times and how his story is one that comes alive, metaphorically, in the world around us and our own lives.

I call heaven and earth to witness against you today that
I have set before you life and death, blessings and curses.
Choose life so that you and your descendants may live.
(Deuteronomy 30:19)

ONE

SEARCHING SELF

Jesus went on with his disciples to the villages of Caesarea Philippi; and on the way he asked his disciples, "Who do people say that I am?" And they answered him, "John the Baptist; and others, Elijah; and still others, one of the prophets." He asked them, "But who do you say that I am?" Peter answered him, "You are the Messiah." And he sternly ordered them not to tell anyone about him. (Mark 8:27–30)

Reflections
BY CAREN

One day between my fifty-first and fifty-sixth birthdays, I looked in the magnifying mirror suction cupped to my medicine cabinet and had no idea who stared back. The shape of what I assumed was still my face had changed. I noticed an eyetooth, carefully flossed, brushed, and otherwise maintained over many years, had shifted. It now pointed east instead of south. Moreover, when that tooth decided to go awry many others foolishly followed like chained links. And what about that itsy-bitsy mole that the black rim of my glasses used to hide? "Not so tiny anymore," I mumbled to myself while frowning at the large, amorphous blob of brown silly putty permanently stuck to my face. "How many people stare at that," I wondered. Beyond the glasses—a necessary concession to failing to read the phone book font during my late forties—sat my right eye. Now stronger progressive bifocal lenses enhanced not only the miniscule tag of skin that began growing on the upper lid between fifty-four and fifty-five but also a dark crater under the lower. A similar circle under my other eye gave new meaning to the expression "mirror image." While turning my face to see whether nose hairs had sprouted and upper lip stubble needed plucking, sunlight poured through the window. Did it brighten my day? Hardly. Instead, it revealed the mysterious overnight development of peach-like fuzz on my right jowl. In despair and disgust, I risked turning the other cheek. As I looked straight ahead with a faux Pollyanna attitude that somehow I would find myself looking at a glass of lemonade half-full, I felt another whack: "Dammit. This stuff is taking over this side also."

For the next half hour, the mug in the mirror taunted me. Like one monkey picking nits off another, I searched every inch of those foreign features for forensic findings that could help me identify and eradicate the source of a liver spot, neck creases destined to become wrinkles and other crimes against my former face. For the first time—or was it the twenty-first?—I harbored thoughts of coloring my curly, wavy, often frizzy salt and pepper hair, buying age-defying creams, and even—for what I now consider a complete loss of sensibility—investing in cosmetic surgery, contact lenses, and bright white porcelain caps.

To set the record straight, I have done none of the above except the following. On the advice of my dentist, a saint with a talent for overriding my genetic disposition to loosing teeth, I periodically consign savings to restoring thirty-year-old crowns on real molars that would otherwise be replaced with false ones. I occasionally pluck unwanted hairs growing where they ought not (to date my ears remain free and clear—although a constant whistle and hearing loss is another story). And I regularly check that the ever-growing silly putty doesn't meet suspicious mole criteria. And that's all. To make any of the other changes pondered would be totally out of character, I tell myself. "It's just not who I am."

Of course today, as I stand before that same truth-telling mirror bemoaning the fact that my sixtieth birthday is history, my seasoned answers to the question, "Who am I?" no longer feel honest. And if that's true, who do I now say I am or am not?

Such questions prompt list making even among those of us who are not anal and will never admit to being old enough to find them necessary for navigating the day. But what kind of lists? Lists of relatives? Schools? Vocations? Avocations? Marriages? Friendships? Disassociations? Residences? Organizations? Affiliations? Triumphs? Tragedies? Failures? Beliefs? Disbeliefs? Regrets? Illnesses? Beginnings? Endings? All of the above? More to come?

Six decades into the process, the tasks of trying to nail down who I am still confound me. Asking my spouse, children, relatives, friends, a mentor, casual acquaintances, professional peers, e-mail correspondents, and even reconnecting with a classmate passing through after forty years doesn't help. They only know who I was before I took my last really good look in the mirror just an hour ago. To the question, "Who do you say I am?" they offer answers built on ancient data, solitary events, psychobabble, first impressions, projections, and those times they heard me say something nice or naughty or nothing at all. They construct who I am based on what they want, need, expect, believe, love, remember, regret, forget, hate, and fear. They answer as though the question is rhetorical and so each time I must consider whether it was.

The last time my mother visited me before she died, I stood with her as she looked in a mirror pointing at her reflection. "Caren. I don't know who that person is," she said. "I don't feel like the seventy-four-year-old staring back at me. Inside I still feel like I'm twenty-five. Okay, maybe forty-five."

"I know just what you mean," I said honestly. "I'm having the same experiences when I look in the mirror."

Standing in the silence that held our shared moment and looking straight ahead, both of us could see a bit more of an answer. I touched the reflection of my nose and then the reflection of hers. Other comparisons followed. I pointed out what was on her face and what would probably appear on mine some day. She touched what was on my face and then showed me where I could find it on hers. We both had a lifelong blemish we couldn't stand in the same place. She had it removed several times, but it always grew back. For me it was a childhood lesson learned and relearned. I never tried getting rid of it. Then there was that way we both tilted our heads. There—before our eyes—right then—we were doing it.

For a few more minutes, we giggled like preteen girls as the game played itself out. We never told anyone about our silliness, and the next time those moments came to mind was the afternoon I delivered the eulogy at my mother's funeral. "Let me tell you about Muriel Oglesby," I said, knowing that the best I could do was to hold up snapshots of her life for those gathered to recall or view them for the first time.

Afterwards, when people came up to express condolences, they said ever so kindly that I had captured who she was. I think not. Indeed, the hours, days, and years that have followed redevelop and enlarge the pictures of her that I cropped into snippets that day. Standing in silence and looking in the mirror alone, I reach out and touch my face while still asking who that mother, grandmother, great-grandmother, wife, ex-wife, friend, cousin, aunt, sister, and neighbor was.

Wonderings and Wanderings

Reread the passage from Mark 8. As it opens, we meet Jesus and the disciples as they are about to enter the villages of Caesarea Philippi. This is a literal and figurative turning point in the story of Jesus' journey from Nazareth in Galilee. These villages are as far north as his ministry of healing, teaching, and preaching will take him before he changes direction and sets his face south toward Jerusalem.

Enter into the story by seeing yourself among those on the road with Jesus. You see him turn to his disciples and hear him ask, "Who do people say I am?"

You begin pondering the reasons why Jesus might ask this question about what people say. The disciples answer that people say Jesus is John the Baptist, Elijah, or one of the prophets. Take time to explore images, memories, thoughts that may come to mind if you remember stories and information about these biblical characters.

- According to the disciples, what are people *not* saying in response to Jesus' question?

Next, Jesus asks his disciples, "But who do you say I am?" You notice that only Peter responds.

- What might be reasons and possibilities for the others' silence?

Stay in character as one traveling with Jesus and draw a line down the middle of a blank piece of paper. On one side, record nouns and phrases to answer the question: "Who do I say Jesus is?" On the other side, write down who, in your eyes, he is not.

In ancient times, Jews believed that the role of the messiah—an anointed one—would be to usher in a messianic age that would change the world. In those days, prophets, priests, and kings were anointed. But rather than endowing one with divinity, anointing was a call to take on a mantle of responsibility and receive the authority to be heard and to even make things happen that would result in "sight for all who were blind" and the "release of all who were captive."

- In your own words, how would you reword Peter's answer to Jesus?

As soon as Peter answers, Jesus "sternly" orders all the disciples not to tell anyone. Definitions of the word *sternly* include rigid, strict, and uncompromising as well as severe and allowing no leeway. Synonyms for the word *sternly* include strictly, harshly, firmly, hardheartedly, unsympathetically, and austerely. The definitions and synonyms just mentioned are for the word *sternly* in English. The original Greek *epitimao* is stronger and means rebuke, sternly admonish, censure, and warn.

- Why do you think Jesus might have reacted this way?
- Jesus responds with neither a yes nor a no. Why?
- If you were to imagine Jesus asking himself the question, "Who do I say I am?" how might he answer his own question?

Go back through the chapters of your life.

- Who along the way in your family, among friends, and in other personal and professional relationships helped to define who you were and who you are?
- Are there ones who never understood who you were, who you aspired to be, who you've become, and who you are becoming?

Stop whatever you are doing and sit quietly, or look in the mirror, or go stand in the midst of a crowded room, mall, or a place away from home and ask yourself, "Who do I say I am?"

Mirrors

I am a victim of my biography.
　　—Barack Obama[4]

In the world to come I shall not be asked, "Why were you not Moses?" I shall be asked, "Why were you not Zusya?"
　　—Rabbi Zusya[5]

Methinks that what they call my shadow here on earth is my true substance.
　　—Herman Melville[6]

I am what I am and that's all that I am. I'm Popeye the Sailor Man.
　　—Popeye

The Idea of Ancestry (I)
by Etheridge Knight[7]

> Taped to the wall of my cell are 47 pictures: 47 black
> faces: my father, mother, grandmothers(1 dead), grand-
> fathers (both dead), brothers, sisters, uncles, aunts,
> cousins (1st and 2nd), nieces, and nephews. They stare
> across the space at me sprawling on my bunk. I know
> their dark eyes, they know mine. I know their style,
> they know mine. I am all of them, they are all of me;
> they are farmers, I am a thief, I am me, they are thee.
>
> I have at one time or another been in love with my mother,
> 1 grandmother, 2 sisters, 2 aunts (1 went to the asylum),
> and 5 cousins. I am now in love with a 7-yr-old niece
> (she sends me letters in large block print, and
> her picture is the only one that smiles at me).
>
> I have the same name as 1 grandfather, 3 cousins, 3 nephews,
> and 1 uncle. The uncle disappeared when he was 15, just took
> off and caught a freight (they say). He's discussed each year
> when the family has a reunion, he causes uneasiness in
> the clan, he is an empty space. My father's mother, who is 93
> and who keeps the Family Bible with everybody's birth dates
> (and death dates) in it, always mentions him. There is no
> place in her Bible for "whereabouts unknown."

Ticket
by Charles O. Hartman[8]

> I love the moment at the ticket window—he says—
> when you are to say the name of your destination, and realize
> that you could say anything, the man at the counter
> will believe you, the woman at the counter
> would never say No, that isn't where you're going,
> you could buy a ticket for one place and go to another,
> less far along the same line. Suddenly you would find yourself
> —he says—in a locality you've never seen before,
> where no one has ever seen you and you could say your name
> was anything you like, nobody would say No,
> that isn't you, this is who you are. It thrills me every time.

Self Portrait
by Edward Hirsch[9]

I lived between my heart and my head,
like a married couple who can't get along.

I lived between my left arm, which is swift
and sinister, and my right, which is righteous.

I lived between a laugh and a scowl,
and voted against myself, a two-party system.

My left leg dawdled or danced along,
my right cleaved to the straight and narrow.

My left shoulder was like a stripper on vacation,
my right stood upright as a Roman soldier.

Let's just say that my left side was the organ
donor and leave my private parts alone,

but as for my eyes, which are two shades
of brown, well, Dionysus, meet Apollo.

Look at Eve raising her left eyebrow
while Adam puts his right foot down.

No one expected it to survive,
but divorce seemed out of the question.

I suppose my left hand and my right hand
will be clasped over my chest in the coffin

and I'll be reconciled at last,
I'll be whole again.

From *A Doll's House*
by Henrik Ibsen[10]

Nora: . . . [W]hen I was at home with papa, he told me his opinion about everything, and so I had the same opinions; and if I differed from him I concealed
the fact, because he would not have liked it. He called me his doll-child, and he
played with me just as I used to play with my dolls. And when I came to live
with you . . .

I mean that I was simply transferred from papa's hands into yours. You
arranged everything according to your own taste, and so I got the same tastes as

you or else I pretended to, I am really not quite sure which—I think sometimes the one and sometimes the other. When I look back on it, it seems to me as if I had been living here like a poor woman—just from hand to mouth. I have existed merely to perform tricks for you, Torvald. But you would have it so. You and papa have committed a great sin against me. It is your fault that I have made nothing of my life.

Helmer: How unreasonable and how ungrateful you are, Nora! Have you not been happy here?

Nora: No, I have never been happy. I thought I was, but it has never really been so . . . only merry. And you have always been so kind to me. But our home has been nothing but a playroom. I have been your doll-wife, just as at home I was papa's doll-child; and here the children have been my dolls. I thought it great fun when you played with me, just as they thought it great fun when I played with them. That is what our marriage has been, Torvald.

Helmer: There is some truth in what you say—exaggerated and strained as your view of it is. But for the future it shall be different. Playtime shall be over, and lesson-time shall begin. . . .

Nora: Alas, Torvald, you are not the man to educate me into being a proper wife for you.

Helmer: And you can say that!

Nora: And I—how am I fitted to bring up the children?

Helmer: Nora!

Nora: Didn't you say so yourself a little while ago—that you dare not trust me to bring them up?

Helmer: In a moment of anger! Why do you pay any heed to that?

Nora: Indeed, you were perfectly right. I am not fit for the task. There is another task I must undertake first. I must try and educate myself—you are not the man to help me in that. I must do that for myself. And that is why I am going to leave you now. . . . I must stand quite alone, if I am to understand myself and everything about me. It is for that reason that I cannot remain with you any longer. . . .

Helmer: To desert your home, your husband and your children! And you don't consider what people will say!

Nora: I cannot consider that at all. I only know that it is necessary for me.

Helmer: It's shocking. This is how you would neglect your most sacred duties.

Nora: What do you consider my most sacred duties?

Helmer: Do I need to tell you that? Are they not your duties to your husband and your children?

Nora: I have other duties just as sacred.

Helmer: That you have not. What duties could those be?

Nora: Duties to myself.

Helmer: Before all else, you are a wife and a mother.

Nora: I don't believe that any longer. I believe that before all else I am a reasonable human being, just as you are—or, at all events, that I must try and become one. I know quite well, Torvald, that most people would think you right, and that views of that kind are to be found in books; but I can no longer content myself with what most people say, or with what is found in books. I must think over things for myself and get to understand them. . . .

Helmer: You talk like a child. You don't understand the conditions of the world in which you live.

Nora: No, I don't. But now I am going to try. I am going to see if I can make out who is right, the world or I.

Helmer: You are ill, Nora; you are delirious; I almost think you are out of your mind.

Nora: I have never felt my mind so clear and certain as tonight.

Helmer: And is it with a clear and certain mind that you forsake your husband and your children?

Nora: Yes, it is.

Helmer: Then there is only one possible explanation.

Nora: What is that?

Helmer: You do not love me anymore.

Nora: No, that is just it . . .

Helmer: And can you tell me what I have done to forfeit your love?

Nora: Yes, indeed I can. It was tonight, when the wonderful thing did not happen; then I saw you were not the man I had thought you were.

Helmer: Explain yourself better. I don't understand you.

Nora: I have waited so patiently for eight years; for, goodness knows, I knew very well that wonderful things don't happen every day. Then this horrible misfortune came upon me; and then I felt quite certain that the wonderful thing was going to happen at last. When Krogstad's letter was lying out there, never for a moment did I imagine that you would consent to accept this man's conditions. I was so absolutely certain that you would say to him: Publish the thing to the whole world. And when that was done—

Helmer: Yes, what then? —when I had exposed my wife to shame and disgrace?

Nora: When that was done, I was so absolutely certain, you would come forward and take everything upon yourself, and say: I am the guilty one.

Helmer: Nora—!

Nora: You mean that I would never have accepted such a sacrifice on your part? No, of course not. But what would my assurances have been worth against yours? That was the wonderful thing which I hoped for and feared; and it was to prevent that, that I wanted to kill myself.

Helmer: I would gladly work night and day for you, Nora—bear sorrow and want for your sake. But no man would sacrifice his honour for the one he loves.

Nora: It is a thing hundreds of thousands of women have done.

Reconciliation
by William S. Cottringer[11]

Living is experiencing
both paths of life—
Peace and turmoil,
right and wrong,
together and alone.

Wisdom is knowing why—
so we can see the difference
and finally find
the hidden path between,
where things rejoin.

We get our share of bruises
searching for this simple truth;
as it is revealed to us
when we don't understand,
loitering and lost,
deaf and blind.

When we do wake up
to knowing who we are,
we start our real journey—
putting back together
all the things we took apart.

TWO

LIVING QUESTIONS

As Jesus passed along the Sea of Galilee, he saw Simon and his brother Andrew casting a net into the sea—for they were fishermen. And Jesus said to them, "Follow me and I will make you fish for people." And immediately they left their nets and followed him. As he went a little farther, he saw James son of Zebedee and his brother John, who were in their boat mending the nets. Immediately he called them; and they left their father Zebedee in the boat with the hired men, and followed him. (Mark 1:16–20)

Reflections

BY TED

"WANTED—something to do for a year or for a lifetime." I tacked the 3 x 5 index card to the bulletin board outside the dining hall. On the one hand I could finish the work on my doctorate in mathematics and have the security of a career in academia. On the other hand . . .

It was "the other hand" that scared me. I had no idea what that might look like. I had a wife and two children to support. In our plans to move from a university town in Tennessee to another one three states away to finish my PhD, we had already sold our house, paid off our bills, and were trying to stretch the little left over. Most days I felt stuck in a psychic tug of war. Yes, on the one hand I could follow the path of least resistance, complete my doctorate, and reap the rewards. Yet, I also knew that despite the payoff, that plan also had some high, frightening costs.

Earlier that year David, a close friend, one-time next door neighbor, and colleague in the English department of the university where we both taught, thrust the door open as I finished up the supper dishes. We hadn't seen each other since celebrating the news that after seven years of writing

and taking oral exams, we could finally dub him "Dr." Startled, I turned
from the sink and stared into his bloodshot eyes. As he began rattling off a
laundry list of frustrating events and his doubts about teaching all his life, I
felt helpless. He couldn't stand still and his fists pounded a disturbing
rhythm on his thighs as he paced back and forth. I still don't remember his
words, but I know nothing I said helped to calm him. David left as agitated
as he had entered and when he pulled the door shut it sounded as though
he wanted to yank it off its hinge. The next morning his wife heard his car
running in the garage. She opened the door and saw a hose stretched from
the tailpipe to a slightly cracked window and knew, instantly, that David lay
dead in the back seat.

David's funeral in the university chapel marked the first time that I
attended a church service since arriving in Tennessee, and the unfamiliar
comfort it offered in the midst of my distress over his suicide surprised
me. After the minister pronounced the final blessing, the other pallbear-
ers and I carried David's coffin on our shoulders out the main doors and
slid it into the waiting hearse. Twenty minutes later, as I listened to the
minister pray and watched mourners weep during the burial service on a
hillside overlooking a river, my heart felt heavier than the box being low-
ered into the ground.

A few weeks of sleepless nights and sorrowful days later, I ran into
Richard, a man who had worked with my father a decade earlier when Pop
was an executive in New York City. "The scuttlebutt in the office was that
your old man was crazy," he said. "Just imagine, six kids with two of them in
college and out of nowhere he decides to give up a successful career with a
major corporation and become a starving artist! Your father did some
strange things with lots of passion. Like that time he converted a school
bus into a camper and drove his family across the country in it. But leaving
DuPont and all that money and the other perks—that was over the top."

I had been a sophomore in college when Pop left the corporate world
and moved our family to the coast of North Carolina so he could paint
watercolor seascapes and run a small gift shop. Now I was in my late twenties, facing the choice of what I wanted to do—"for a year or for a lifetime." For the first time, I realized that when Pop left DuPont he made a
choice—a difficult choice between hanging onto his secure career or listening to his heart's call to do what he loved.

Although I sensed that David's death had thrown me onto a path that
was beginning to diverge from the secure and the known, I felt clueless as
to why and where it all might lead. Unlike Pop, I didn't know what I loved
and didn't feel passionate about anything. All I did know was that I no

longer felt confident about spending my life in academia. My family responsibilities jerked me toward security, but my heart and soul kept tugging me toward something else. But what?

As the spring semester ended, we packed up our household, and I still struggled with the unanswered question: "So what's next, Ted?" From five hundred miles away my folks, aware of my despair over David's death and confusion about my future, invited me to join them for a week in the mountains of North Carolina at an Episcopal Church conference center. It was there that I posted my "WANTED" ad outside the dining hall, and it was in those days that an Episcopal priest mentioned seminary and spoke of being "called."

"On the one hand I could continue my work on a doctorate in mathematics," I said to that priest. "On the other hand . . ." I drew a blank. I didn't know how to end the sentence. I didn't know where or what "the other hand" was, or if I even really understood what a seminary was. I didn't know if everything I planned was what I was "called" to do, or whether it was just convenient. "After all," I told him. "It's not like I have a whole lot of experience with being a part of a church community, or that I can even tell you what my 'faith' is about."

"Think about it," he replied. "We'll talk again."

"On the other hand . . ." Throughout the rest of the conference, Pop's decision so many years before began stirring and churning something deep inside. To do or not to do became a battle between my mind and my soul that wearied my sensibilities. For someone who hadn't gone to church in years, I soon found myself praying all the time—simple childhood prayers and the psalms and my own words and in them I found a calming release from the tension of opposing forces.

The decision didn't come easily but within a week of leaving the conference I felt ready to pack up my family and go to seminary. However, others weren't so sure. Every time I thought I had figured out all the "what to do" and "how to do it" scenarios concerning finances and logistics, my wife would cautiously counter with another. Each created new anxieties that needed to be tackled in long conversations where we didn't necessarily agree to disagree with each other. Often, angry words and tears spilled out and over before hugs and mutual reassurances could follow.

I then spent the rest of the summer realizing that my decision to go to seminary was only part of a balanced equation to get there. I needed to be stamped with approval after long meetings with the clergy from my home parish, the vestry, a diocesan committee, and finally the bishop. I also found myself concerned about a physical and sweating over an evaluation by a psychiatrist. Finally, the day for the interview with the dean and faculty at the seminary arrived, followed by weeks of impatient waiting to hear if they were convinced that what I said I wanted matched what they said and wanted. As I waded anxiously through those weeks, I often found myself in a familiar swamp, grappling anew with doubts about leaving academia and my abiding grief and growing anger over David's path out of it.

By the time I got to seminary, I realized that although I knew little about what caused Pop to awaken to his soul's struggle, David's suicide was responsible for mine. On the day my father left DuPont for the last time, he prayed his choice would result in new life for him and his family. On a warm September morning, as I headed for orientation in the seminary chapel, I thought of Pop, wondered for the ten thousandth time how I had gotten myself into this, said a short prayer, and swallowed hard. Steps away from the massive wooden doors, I turned to run for my life, but just then something stopped me and I found myself smiling like an excited little boy who just won a tug of war. Entering the sanctuary, I knew that for the first time since David died, I was alive.

Wonderings and Wanderings

In this passage Jesus calls two sets of brothers to "follow" him. Simon and his brother Andrew are "casting nets." James and his brother John are "mending nets." As you think about these jobs, describe them and the ways, in today's world, that people "cast" and "mend" their nets.

Jesus' invitation to Simon and Andrew is a clever play—on words. They obediently follow, just as James and John did. Name some of the tugs and pulls that would have pushed them to follow Jesus, and those that would have yanked them back to continuing to "cast" or "mend" their nets.

"Immediately he called them."

- Outside of a religious or institutional church setting, who or what calls people like you and me?
- What might we be called out of, or called into, or called to do, or called to be, or even called not to do, or not to be?
  - How do we discern where a call comes from or who calls us? External signs of a call might be? And the signs in our hearts or souls that indicate that we hear a call?
- What obstacles appear that can distort, confuse, or impede this discernment?

- Once we hear a call, what forces influence people like you and me and keep us from responding?
- And what are the forces, both external and internal, that have the power to pull us away from "casting" and "mending" to follow the call?

Name the nets that you "cast' and "mend" daily.

- Do other forces call you in another direction?
- If so, why do you continue to cast and mend?
- What might the promise be?
  - What might be the promise of abandoning your nets to follow a calling?
  - And what might the cost be?
- What resources could you employ to discern which path you might choose to follow?

Mirrors

Lord, take me where you want me to go;
Let me meet who you want me to meet;
Tell me what you want me to say
And keep me out of your way.
—Mychal Judge, NYFD chaplain who died on 9/11[12]

Vocation is not a goal to be achieved but a gift to be received.
—Parker Palmer[13]

Follow the grain in your own wood.
—Howard Thurman[14]

A career seeks to be successful, a calling to be valuable. A career tries to make money, a calling tries to make a difference.
—William Sloane Coffin[15]

Do not go by revelation or tradition, do not go by rumor, or the sacred scriptures, do not go by hearsay or mere logic, do not go by bias towards a notion or by another person's seeming ability and do not go by the idea "He is our teacher." But when you yourself know that a thing is good, that it is not blamable, that is praised by the wise and when practiced and observed that it leads to happiness, then follow that thing.
—Buddha[16]

The Night House
by Billy Collins[17]

Every day the body works in the fields of the world
mending a stone wall
or swinging a sickle through the tall grass—-
the grass of civics, the grass of money—
and every night the body curls around itself
and listens for the soft bells of sleep.

But the heart is restless and rises
from the body in the middle of the night,
leaves the trapezoidal bedroom
with its thick, pictureless walls
to sit by herself at the kitchen table
and heat some milk in a pan.

And the mind gets up too, puts on a robe
and goes downstairs, lights a cigarette,
and opens a book on engineering.
Even the conscience awakens
and roams from room to room in the dark,
darting away from every mirror like a strange fish.

And the soul is up on the roof
in her nightdress, straddling the ridge,
singing a song about the wildness of the sea
until the first rip of pink appears in the sky.
Then, they all will return to the sleeping body
the way a flock of birds settles back into a tree,
resuming their daily colloquy,
talking to each other or themselves
even through the heat of the long afternoons.
Which is why the body—that house of voices—
sometimes puts down its metal tongs, its needle, or its pen
to stare into the distance,

to listen to all its names being called
before bending again to its labor.

[W]e might step back and wonder if doing what God is calling us to do is always a matter of doing that for which we are best qualified. Certainly the Bible records numerous instances in which this was emphatically not the case. . . . After all, a stuttering Moses was called by God to speak before Pharaoh; Jonah was instructed to call the city of Nineveh to repentance, a city he himself would have liked to see burn under God's judgment; and the personally unimpressive Paul was prevailed upon to present the gospel to the entire Gentile world. It seems unlikely that a modern vocational counseling agency would have directed these biblical characters to their respective tasks on the basis of their native interests and talents.

—Mark Schwein and Dorothy Bass, *Leading Lives that Matter: What We Should Do and Who We Should Be*[18]

From "Serving God"
by Andrew Longmore[19]

She is Sister Andrea now, where once she was just Andrea Jaeger, tennis wonderkid. Where once she would get up to hit tennis balls at dawn, now she begins her day in prayer. Where once her life was bordered by the lines on a tennis court, now it is limited only by the hours in the day. "Sometimes," she says with a laugh, "I look at my 'to do' list in the morning and know that it would take four miracles to achieve it all, not just one."

At the age of 41 and nearly two decades after her enforced retirement from the game, Jaeger does not sound at all daunted by the prospect. Three months ago she was ordained a sister of the Order of Dominican Nuns in the Episcopal Church. . . . It has been a long, sometimes tortuous, often uplifting journey of sacrifice on the road to a destiny she dimly glimpsed as an impressionable teenager lost in an adult world.

Along the way she had to reconcile a stormy relationship with her overbearing father, Roland, and admit to losing matches on purpose, among them the Wimbledon final of 1983. Through a painful and all too brief childhood, Jaeger discovered she had few equals at hitting tennis balls, but lacked the killer instinct required of great champions; that sometimes she hated herself for beating less gifted opponents. In her junior days in Chicago, an opponent committed suicide after a defeat. In the women's locker-room, inhabited by Chris Evert, Billie Jean King and Martina Navratilova, the 15-year-old found herself out of step with a ruthlessly competitive environment. Victory was acclaimed by her parents and the public, but not in her soul.

"I didn't join the circuit to be No. 1," she says. "I didn't join the tennis circuit to grow up to be a professional tennis player. I joined because I was good enough to, and there were aspects I loved and aspects that haunted me." She also played the game to please her parents. . . . "I was sitting in my hotel room all night going, 'Well, everybody thinks I'm great because I won, but what about the person I beat? How's she feeling?' I was tormented."

. . . She played sporadically in the following years, still suffering the pain from an injured shoulder, and returned briefly to the Tour and retired in 1987. Rex Bellamy, the *Times* tennis correspondent, believed that Evonne Goolagong often lost in finals because her main incentive for winning was to play another match. Jaeger's incentive for losing was partly spiritual, partly emotional. She minded losing less than her opponent. Only three years ago, though, did Jaeger admit to "tanking" in the final of the 1983 Wimbledon Championships, a tournament she had blasted through without losing a set. On the eve of the final, after a protracted row with her father, she was shut out of the family's rented house in Wimbledon. Jaeger went to knock on the door of the only person she knew in the street, which happened to be Navratilova. The next day the three-time champion finished Jaeger off in 54 minutes.

"I want to be truthful and to be able to look at myself in the mirror," she said. "I never wanted to be disrespectful of the traditions and history of Wimbledon, but life is more important than a tennis match and you say thank you in the only way you know how. . . . I never looked back on my tennis career until this year and I've never wondered how good I could have been," she says. "If I'd have stayed out there for 10 years and not been injured and won all the Grand Slams, I think I would have lost a bit of my soul. Professional tennis was my teenage calling; this is my adult calling. When my teenage years were done, it was time to move on to something else."

By Rainer Maria Rilke
(trans. Robert Bly)[20]

> I love the dark hours of my being
> in which my senses drop into the deep.
> I have found in them, as in old letters,
> my private life, that is already lived through,
> and become wide and powerful now, like legends.
> Then I know that there is room in me
> for a second huge and timeless life.
>
> But sometimes I am like the tree that stands
> over a grave, a leafy tree, fully grown,
> who has lived out that particular dream, that the dead boy
> (around whom its warm roots are pressing)
> lost through his sad moods and his poems.

What We Want
by Linda Pastan[21]

> What we want
> is never simple.
> We move among the things
> we thought we wanted:
> a face, a room, an open book
> and these things bear our names—
> now they want us.
> But what we want appears
> in dreams, wearing disguises.
> We fall past,
> holding out our arms
> and in the morning
> our arms ache.
> We don't remember the dream,
> but the dream remembers us.
> It is there all day
> as an animal is there
> under the table,
> as the stars are there
> even in full sun.

Internal Exile
by Richard Cecil[22]

Although most people I know were condemned
years ago by Judge Necessity
to life in condos near a freeway exit
convenient to their twice-a-day commutes
through traffic jams to jobs that they dislike,
they didn't bury their heads in their hands
and cry "Oh, no!" when sentence was pronounced.
Forty years of accounting in Duluth!
or *Tenure at Southwest Missouri State!*
Instead, they mumbled, *not bad. It could be worse,*
when the bailiff, Fate, led them away
to Personnel to fill out payroll forms
and have their smiling ID photos snapped.
And that's what they still mumble every morning
just before their snooze alarms go off
when Fluffy nuzzles them out of their dreams
of making out with movie stars on beaches.
They rise at five a.m. and feed their cats
and drive to work and work and drive back home
and feed their cats and eat and fall asleep
while watching Evening News's fresh disasters—
blown-up bodies littering a desert
fought over for the last three thousand years,
and smashed-to-pieces million-dollar houses
built on islands swept by hurricanes.
It's soothing to watch news about the places
where people literally will die to live
when you live someplace with no attractions—
mountains, coastline, history—like here,
where none aspire to live, though many do.
"A great place to work, with no distractions"
is how my interviewer first described it
nineteen years ago, when he hired me.
And, though he moved the day that he retired
to his dream house in the uplands with a vista,
he wasn't lying—working's better here
and easier than trying to have fun.
Is that the way it is where you're stuck, too?

THREE

FACING FEAR

Immediately he made the disciples get into the boat and go on ahead to the other side, while he dismissed the crowds. And after he had dismissed the crowds, he went up the mountain by himself to pray. When evening came, he was there alone, but by this time the boat, battered by the waves, was far from the land, for the wind was against them. And early in the morning he came walking toward them on the sea. But when the disciples saw him walking on the sea, they were terrified, saying, "It is a ghost!" And they cried out in fear. But immediately Jesus spoke to them and said, "Take heart, it is I; do not be afraid."

Peter answered him, "Lord, if it is you, command me to come to you on the water." He said, "Come." So Peter got out of the boat, started walking on the water, and came toward Jesus. But when he noticed the strong wind, he became frightened, and beginning to sink, he cried out, "Lord, save me!" Jesus immediately reached out his hand and caught him, saying to him, "You of little faith, why did you doubt?" When they got into the boat, the wind ceased. (Matthew 14:22–32)

Reflections
BY CAREN

Like many television programs, the Weather Channel can become an addiction. Indeed, in our household the reporter on that station often feels like a neighbor who joins my husband daily for breakfast, periodic coffee breaks, dinner, bedtime, and at other randomly chosen hours. My daughter reports that the same "man (or woman) who came for dinner" phenomenon also takes place in her bedroom, family room, or home office at regular intervals. Although both of us name this predictable occurrence "a guy thing" and place responsibility for it on our husbands, we also admit getting hooked ourselves.

I would like to think that living in Florida provides ample excuses for the occasional over-focus on weather reports—at least during hurricane season when the Boy Scout motto "be prepared" rules. As for the other six months of the year—conditions for playing golf or going to the beach suffice as a justification for a.m. and p.m. updates. However, the truth is most of our rationalizations are lame and our interest in the weather was the same when we lived in the north with lake-effect snow, Canadian clippers, ice storms, and wind chill factors plummeting thermometers below zero.

No doubt, weather forecasts popping up on our televisions, computer screens, and cell phones save lives. But what has this technology to scientifically predict the future with assurances and reassurances done to our natural instincts to "feel" impending storms, read skies and roads ahead with a sense of awe and mystery, smell rain before it falls, hear stillness signaling impending change, and trust our innate resources to find or create safe harbors for ourselves in the midst of unforeseen events?

The moment my fingers found a lump that claimed squatter's rights in my left breast, the realization that all was not well wiped out the sense of security I'd felt six weeks before after a radiologist reported a clean mammogram. Instantly, the warm, gentle shower rinsing my soapy torso did nothing to stop the sudden heart-stopping freeze that twisted my gut like a soaked towel getting wrung out. I don't know how long I stood motionless as water poured off and around me, but when I could finally move again the first of many reality checks followed. But no matter how I approached evacuation routes from the storm brewing in my brain and churning in my gut, my walking fingers always wound up in the same spot—a hard, unmapped protuberance that pointed to unpredictable currents, battering waves, and possibly life-threatening consequences ahead.

In the days, then weeks, that followed I saw doctor after doctor. I took one test after another. The doctor doing the first test said, "Let's try this and wait three weeks to see if it goes away." We tried and waited and nothing changed and the stormy weather conditions loomed as I drove to see my newest doctor.

"Please tell me it's all right," I said to myself, to my husband, and to God as the car inched toward the appointed hour. However, the sonogram the surgeon administered replied to those pleas with turbulent news. "Trust me," he said. "We'll deal with this one step at a time and you will be okay." The next time we spoke was on my way to have a biopsy. A week later his voice on the other end of the phone reported I had cancer. "But it is so small we can get it all," he assured me. I know more than that was said, but the lab report instantly became a tornado that whirled through my head, knocked my positive outlook into oblivion, and shattered every word that followed.

The truth and its consequences have a special way of shredding our egos and putting us in our place. For years I wrote for national magazines and daily newspapers about holistic health, complementary medicine, and what people should do to gain a degree of self-control when they were ill and feeling out of control. I was so good at it that I even wrote a book on the subject for a famous doctor. However, now all those wise words and years of experience felt foreign. My world was that strange, out-of-control one, and I didn't know where I could find sparkling red shoes to click together three times, a magic wand, forgiveness for any specific sins that caused cancer, or whatever else that could get me back to where I was before getting a life-threatening weather report.

During the days before my surgery to clean up the site of the tumor removed for biopsy and make sure the cancer had not spread, my quest to discover who would save me from my fears and counter my doubts stretched from my husband, children, and doctors to friends, relatives, and members of my spiritual communities. Each one did the best that he or she could to listen, be compassionate, and pray for and with me. Yet despite their efforts and mine, nothing miraculously caused my Tsunami sized waves of emotional distress or the cancer to go away. And all my right answers, suggestions, and advice to others who had ever been in my rocky sinking boat felt like big lies.

The winds of change did come—later, much, much later. Not with every one of my doctors' forecasts of sunny days ahead. Not with the first, second, third, or even fourth annual report that the days of turbulence and devastation were history and I was cancer free. Not with the statistics that said my cure rate was as good as it gets with breast cancer. No, the change came in its own unpredictable way, just like the blessed calm after many a major storm. It came gradually. It came as one ray of sun after another began to peek through lingering black clouds. It came as those little setting-sun pale rainbows called Sun Dogs that frame dark clouds. And at last it became the realization that when I found the lump, reported it, and decided not to let my doubts render me powerless, I could at last take a leap of faith that would carry me to the other side of my darkest hours and worst fears. A leap of faith that still feels like a miracle.

Wonderings and Wanderings

The story about Jesus in Matthew's Gospel opens after King Herod orders John the Baptist to be decapitated. Herod had imprisoned John, the one who baptized Jesus, after the Baptist criticized the monarch for having an affair and marrying his brother Phillip's wife. Jesus' disciples get the news, claim John's body, and bury him before telling Jesus that John is dead. In response, Jesus seeks time alone in a deserted place. However, the crowds hear about this and follow him. Jesus responds by ministering to the sick, and despite the disciples' pleas to send them away, he tells them instead to feed the crowd. When the disciples complain that there is not enough food and they have only five loaves and two fish, Jesus assures them otherwise, blesses the food, and all get fed. As the story that follows opens, Jesus once again tries to find solitude. He sends the disciples away in a boat and then he goes up a mountain to pray.

Put yourself in Jesus' place and see this story as though it were a movie. Focus on the scene where Jesus gets the news that John, whom some said (in the Gospel of Luke) was a cousin, whom many considered a prophet as dynamic as Elijah (whom some considered—and some still consider—to be the Messiah), and with whom Jesus had a profoundly spiritual and intimate encounter at the Jordan River, has been murdered for speaking his truth.

Remember a time and place when you received news of the unexpected death of a leader, teacher, mentor, or relative whom you respected for his or her ideals, values, ethics, or truth-telling. What were

- the first words you thought or said on learning that this person had died unexpectedly?
- the feelings that swirled from your heart throughout your body to your head and the tips of your fingers and toes?
- the places you wanted to go, things you wanted to do next, and people whom you wanted to see and talk to or not see and talk to?

See the disciples as they move far from the shore in a boat. The weather conditions begin to change when evening comes, and the disciples, now alone, find themselves battered by waves, with the wind against them.

- As the sea becomes more turbulent, what might they be saying to one another about Jesus? Being left without him? The day's events? Being far from land? The wind against them? The battering waves?

After a long night, morning comes, and upon seeing Jesus walking on the sea toward them, the disciples become terrified. They believe they are seeing a ghost. As he approaches, Jesus says, "Take heart" and "do not be afraid." Peter replies, "Lord, if it is you, command me to come to you on the water." Jesus replies, "Come."

- How do you hear Peter's statement: "Lord, if it is you, command me to come to you on the water"?
  - Is this a challenge? If so, why might Peter present it?
  - Is this a request? If so, why might Peter make it?
- How might you rewrite Peter's odd statement to Jesus and what he is really asking for?

Peter sets out on the water to meet Jesus, but, noticing the strong wind, he becomes frightened, begins to sink, and calls out to Jesus to save him.

- Although Peter's motive to walk on the water is not revealed, what do you know of garnering up courage to do something unknown, entering into the process of doing it, becoming frightened in the face of strong wind, and finding yourself sinking after setting out?
- Who have you called to—either silently or aloud—to "save" you?
  - What did you want or expect this person to do?

Describe the positive and negative aspects of the power that doubt has had during fearful and challenging times in your life.

- And the power the strong wind had over you during those times?

Jesus refers to "little faith."

- In the context of this story, what does Jesus imply about faith?
- How would you define "faith" during such times in your life?
  - And the ways in which doubt and faith are related?
- When calm came after a time of adverse wind and battering waves, what more did you know about your faith (and your "little" faith), and even doubt, that you didn't know before?

The wise man in the storm prays to God, not for safety from danger, but for deliverance from fear. It is the storm within that endangers him, not the storm without.
—Ralph Waldo Emerson[23]

If everyone woke up tomorrow morning and said, "It's possible; whatever it is, it's possible," and spent a whole day having an "it's possible" day, then we would be going down the kind of road I'm interested in—because I do believe it is possible.
—John Bird[24]

Fear is implanted in us as a preservative from evil; but its duty, like that of other passions, is not to overbear reason, but to assist it. It should not be suffered to tyrannize in the imagination, to raise phantoms of horror, or to beset life with supernumerary distresses.
—Samuel Johnson[25]

Progress always involves risk; you can't steal second base and keep your feet on first.
—Frederick Wilcox[26]

If a man wants something he's never had before, he has to do something he's never done before.
—Crossover, from the movie *Gridiron Gang*[27]

Faith is not only a matter of quantity. In a different way, it's a matter of quality. What does faith mean? Perhaps it means nothing. And for many people it's then what I call an empty shell.
—Rabbi Adin Steinsaltz[28]

From the movie *Walk the Line*[29]

After cutting a record in a do-it-yourself studio, Johnny Cash takes it to a recording studio.

Studio owner: Hold on. Hold on. I hate to interrupt, but you guys got something else? (Pause) I'm sorry. I can't market Gospel no more.
Cash: So that's it?

Owner: I don't record material that doesn't sell, Mr. Cash. And Gospel like that doesn't sell.

Cash: Is it the Gospel or the way I sing it?

Owner: Both.

Cash: What's wrong with the way I sing it?

Owner: I don't believe you.

Cash: You saying I don't believe in God? I want to understand. I mean we come down here and play for a minute and he tells me I don't believe in God.

Owner: You know exactly what I'm telling you. We've already heard that song a hundred times, just like that—just like how you sang it.

Cash: But you didn't let us bring it home.

Owner: OK. Let's bring it home. Mr. Cash, if you were hit by a truck and you was laying out in that gutter and you had time to sing one song—one song people would remember before you're dirt—one song that would let God know what you felt about your time here on earth—one song that would sum you up, you telling me that's the song you'd sing—that same Jimmy Davis tune we hear on the radio all day—about peace within and how it's real and how you're going to shout it? Or would you sing something different—something real—something you feel? Because I'm telling you right now that this is the kind of song people want to hear. That's the kind of song that truly saves people. It ain't got nothing to do with believing in God, Mr. Cash, it has to do with believing in yourself.

Cash: Well, I got a couple of songs I wrote in the Air Force.

From *My Grandfather's Blessings*
by Rachel Naomi Remen[30]

A woman with metastatic cancer once told me that through the experience of her illness she had discovered a basic truth. There are only two kinds of people in this world—those who are alive and those who are afraid. She had smiled at me and said that many of the people she had met who were afraid were doctors.

Perhaps such fear is a natural outcome of the wish to be in control. A patient whose physician told him several years ago that he had three months to live told me in bewilderment that the doctor had seemed "satisfied" as he made this heart-stopping statement. "He seemed sorry to be telling me this but he seemed pleased that he had the information to give me, almost as pleased as if he had told me that he had the right drug to eradicate my cancer. He told me of my death with an air of authority as if it were he who had decided when it would be and in doing so had somehow gained mastery over it as if when he could not control my cancer, he could at least control the time of my death. I was angry for a long time, but I now think he was out of control and vulnerable as I was. Too bad we could not have talked man to man on that level instead of reaching for a false certainty."

Perhaps the most basic skill of the physician is the ability to have comfort with uncertainty, to recognize with humility the uncertainty inherent in all situations, to be open to the ever-present possibility of the surprising, the mysterious, and even the holy, and to meet people there.

The need for certainty is not just a problem for medical professionals. We wish for certainty as ardently as our doctors do, are seduced by it as profoundly and are as disappointed with the uncertain nature of the world. We all yearn for mastery. But mastery is always limited. Sooner or later we will come to the edge of all that we can control and find life, waiting there for us.

The wish to control floats like a buoy above the hidden reef of fear. More than any single thing, fear is the stumbling block to life's agenda. Perhaps it is only the things we fear that we wish to control. No one can serve life if they are unconsciously afraid of life. Life is a process. When he was very old, Roberto Assagioli, the founder of psychosynthesis, reminded one of his young students of this; "There is no certainty; there is only adventure," he told this young man. "Even stars explode."

First Lesson
by Philip Booth[31]

> Lie back, daughter, let your head
> be tipped back in the cup of my hand.
> Gently, and I will hold you. Spread
> your arms wide, lie out on the stream
> and look high at the gulls. A dead-
> man's-float is face down. You will dive
> and swim soon enough where this tidewater
> ebbs to the sea. Daughter, believe
> me, when you tire on the long thrash
> to your island, lie up, and survive.
> As you float now, where I held you
> and let go, remember when fear
> cramps your heart what I told you:
> lie gently and wide to the light-year
> stars, lie back, and the sea will hold you.

FOUR

PAYING ATTENTION

Now as they went on their way, he entered a certain village, where a woman named Martha welcomed him into her home. She had a sister named Mary, who sat at the Lord's feet and listened to what he was saying. But Martha was distracted by her many tasks; so she came to him and asked, "Lord, do you not care that my sister has left me to do all the work by myself? Tell her then to help me." But the Lord answered her, "Martha, Martha, you are worried and distracted by many things; there is need of only one thing. Mary has chosen the better part, which will not be taken away from her." (Luke 10:38–42)

Reflections
BY TED

As I stepped over the puddle to get into the car, I noticed that I was wearing my brown penny loafers with my dark gray suit. Annoyed with myself I went back inside and pulled my black wingtips out of the closet. Not only were the shoes wrong but so were the mismatched socks. After changing them I took one last look in the mirror and realized I was wearing the wrong belt. Now aware that I was beginning to run late, I took off my belt. However, I still couldn't go before changing not only the belt, but from a white button down shirt and tie into a black clergy shirt with a white clerical collar. By the time I pulled out of the driveway, I had delayed myself another half hour, and tears welled up as I turned onto the highway heading toward the hospital.

Just a week earlier I couldn't have cared less about my wardrobe. That night—in the middle of the night—my ex-wife Linda and I threw on jeans, t-shirts, and sandals to rush to the emergency room. Minutes earlier a policeman called to tell us our thirteen-year-old son Christopher had been injured in an auto accident. During the long hours in the waiting room, we learned diagnosis by diagnosis that Christopher had suffered a traumatic head injury along with multiple broken bones. Now, he still hovered at the edge of death—motionless and unresponsive in a coma, in the neuro-intensive care unit.

The accident and Christopher's precarious hold on life shook us to the core and broke our helpless hearts. Grandparents, aunts, uncles, friends, parishioners, and clergy colleagues swarmed to the hospital to surround us with their prayers and presence. With a hospital chaplain's help, we set up camp in a corner of the surgical waiting room and spent the fretful hours between our allotted ten-minute visits with Christopher greeting well-wishers and waiting for the medical staff to give us updates on his condition. Generous supporters brought us hamburgers, pizza, and Chinese takeout to eat off paper plates. At night, exhausted by the vigil, we sought sleep on the worn waiting room sofas under flimsy hospital blankets.

"We've been at the hospital three nights and I'm as grungy as it gets," I told Linda. "Besides, I have to get some things done at home."

"You go. I'm staying here," she replied. "I don't want to leave Christopher."

It wasn't just that I needed a shower and some clean clothes, but there was the mail to pick up, bills to pay, and the trash to take out for pickup. It was the middle of the summer and the lawn needed to be mowed, and the timer set for the sprinkler. On the way home I stopped to fill a prescription, pick up toothbrushes and toothpaste to keep at the hospital, wander up and down supermarket aisles for snacks to take back, and fill the gas tank. My folks had been staying at a motel, but were going to move to our house so I cleaned up the guest bedroom, ran the vacuum, straightened up the kitchen, and swept the porch. I did as much as I could in a few short hours. Then I quickly shaved and showered. Before leaving to go back to the hospital, I went to the front door to get and sort the mail, ran a load of laundry and left a note for my mother to put it in the dryer. Finally I headed for the car—only to be detoured by a gray suit and brown shoes.

Finally behind the wheel, I turned on the radio. Although words from the news broadcast tried to reach my ears, all I heard was gibberish as anxious thoughts dashed from painful memories of the past few days to nightmarish fears of Christopher's prognosis. In the hospital parking lot I sat immobilized. Then, when dread over the questions I now faced for taking so long at home became ridiculous, I grabbed the bag I packed with Linda's change of clothes, locked the car, and went through the revolving door.

"Ted!" called a voice from across the hospital lobby. I turned to see Bob Estill, the bishop of my diocese, a good friend and mentor, coming toward me. "I came as soon as I could," he said. "I was at a meeting in New York when I got the news. I tried calling, but no one picked up. All of you have been in my prayers, and the prayers of those I was with." He then looked at me with an expression of curiosity and surprise. "You look like you're going to visit a hospitalized parishioner." Not waiting for a response he added, "Tell me how he's doing. What do the doctors say?"

We walked together to the elevator as I recounted the accident, the night in the emergency room, and Christopher's extensive injuries. "The doctor says that the swelling is cutting off the blood flow to parts of his brain and that it will kill some tissue, or worse . . . it may kill him. If he survives the next few days they'll do surgery for his broken bones and put him in a body cast for five or six months." The elevator doors opened in front of the surgical waiting room as Bob put his hand on my shoulder, "And how are you doing?" When others asked the same question, I always responded, "As good as to be expected." I gave him the same rote answer, but for some reason—perhaps his touch—something unexpectedly stirred in me that began to leak through a crack in my armor. Catching myself on the verge of a new round of tears, I added, "Why don't you go ahead up to see Linda. Tell her I'll be right there." Sensing I was wobbling on a vulnerable edge, Bob offered, "Why don't we go to the chapel for a few minutes before we see the others in the waiting room?"

"Not now. Maybe later." Surprised at how forceful I sounded, I added, "I've got to get these things to Linda. I'll be there as soon as I visit the restroom."

The picture in the mirror wasn't pretty. My bloodshot, swollen eyes and the rest of my appearance revealed more than I cared for others to know. "Have my eyes been like that since I came in the hospital?" I wondered. "And are those tear stains on my black shirt too?" I also noticed that my suit jacket hung oddly on my slumping shoulders and my rumpled handkerchief half hung out of my pants pocket. As I tucked my shirt into my pants, I found myself hitching my belt one notch tighter than usual. Annoyed that I didn't bring a comb, I wet my hands and tried to brush my unruly head of hair with them. Finally, convinced I could never pull myself back together just right, I left.

I entered the waiting room and immediately took note that no one had watered the flowers or straightened up the magazines, get-well cards, letters, and half-eaten food that littered every surface. Linda and Bob stood side-by-side with bowed heads praying in one corner of our homesteaded quarters while her parents, my parents, and some friends listened, nodded, and whispered. Everyone, including Bob, looked as though they'd been crying. The scene felt like a movie, not my life. Linda, I thought, looked more disheveled than I'd ever seen her . . . coffee stains on the t-shirt she hadn't changed for three days, her uncombed hair a mess, no makeup, a missing earring, barefoot.

"Ted!" she exclaimed. "Ted, Ted, you missed it—you missed it. Christopher squeezed my finger! He squeezed my finger when I sat down next to him to pray. He heard me say 'I love you,' and he squeezed my finger. He knew I was there. He knew it. The nurse saw it. I didn't imagine it. Oh, Ted. I wish you had been here. It's a miracle. It's the one thing we've been asking for—a sign—just some small sign that he's going to make it."

Before leaving, the bishop said more prayers that gave thanks for God's gifts—evidence of Christopher's healing, the staff and doctors at the hospital, the prayers and support of so many near and far. He then petitioned God that Linda and I and our families would continue to have strength for the days ahead. We shared the last "Amen" with the hospital's PA system announcing that our ten-minute window to visit Christopher had opened. Linda and I said quick goodbyes and headed for the NICU while she kept saying, "Oh Ted, I wish you had been there. . . ." As I held open the thick metal door, she suddenly stopped and looked as if she were seeing me for the very first time. "So, what's with the suit?" she asked.

Wonderings and Wanderings

"In those days," Martha, a first-century Jewish woman, had her own home. Consider what this suggests about her. Now see Martha as she watches Jesus enter her village and welcomes him into her home.

- As Jesus moves toward the entrance, how might Martha look and feel?
  - And what might her expectations be of this encounter with Jesus?

Many tasks and worries distract Martha. Name them and what they seemingly distract her from.

- In what ways might those distractions have served Martha?

Assuming that an inner Martha and Mary play roles, come alive, and direct *your* life at certain times and under certain circumstances, wonder about times when one or the other dominates your world.

- How do you use *many tasks*—working extra hours, housecleaning, shopping, preparing food, attending meetings, mowing the lawn, washing the car, managing finances, or even attending social events— as ways to be *distracted*?
- Is there a known risk you might have to take, or a fear you would have to face, or a worry you would have to set aside, or an anxiety you would have to manage if you weren't *distracted*?
- Are there times when your inner "Martha's" approach to hospitality truly serves you and makes you feel welcome and comfortable in certain circumstances?
  - When does her busyness cause you to resent or be annoyed and even angry with others who do not share your concerns, worries, anxieties?
- And Mary—when and how does she come into the picture and allow you to sit and listen?

Mary sat at Jesus' feet and listened to what he was saying. When Martha complains to him about her sister, he replies: *there is need of only one thing.* To what might Jesus be referring?

- When given opportunities to welcome a voice that knows more about that *one thing* and may speak of it, how have your tasks, worries, and other distractions taken over, controlled the moment, and prevented you from listening?
- Why do the distractions that run on auto-pilot within you have that power?
  - When did they claim it?
- Who or what can stop you from being distracted and transform you from a *human doing* into a *human being* who makes time to quietly listen with focused attention?

Throughout the story, Mary and Martha never speak to each other and Mary says nothing while she listens to Jesus. Retell this story from Mary's perspective. If Martha and Mary were to have a conversation after Jesus leaves, what might each say to the other?

Mirrors

Most of our conflicts and difficulties come from trying to deal with the spiritual and practical aspects of our life separately instead of realizing them as parts of one whole. If our practical life is centered on our own interests, cluttered up by possessions, distracted by ambitions, passions, wants and worries, beset by a sense of our own rights and importance, or anxieties for our own future, or longings for our own success, we need not expect that our spiritual life will be a contrast to all this.
　　—Evelyn Underhill[32]

　　The wren—
　　looking here, looking there.
　　You lose something?
　　　　—Issa[33]

A crust eaten in peace is better than a banquet partaken in anxiety.
　　—Aesop[34]

The quality of one's life depends on the quality of attention. Whatever you pay attention to will grow more important in your life.
　　—Deepak Chopra[35]

Worry is a thin stream of fear trickling through the mind. If encouraged, it cuts a channel into which all other thoughts are drained.
　　—Arthur Somers Roche[36]

Worry often gives a small thing a big shadow.
　　—Swedish Proverb[37]

Worry never teaches us anything useful. When we worry we disempower ourselves and lessen our trust in God. When we worry, our anxiety mounts as we manipulate everyone around us to make room for our worry and to accommodate our anxiety.
　　—Holly Whitcomb[38]

**From *The Zen Commandments: Ten Suggestions
for a Life of Inner Freedom***
by Dean Sluyter[39]

One morning I found myself running through the Newark, New Jersey
train station, trying to make a connection to New York, dodging frantically
through the crowd as complex scenarios of missed appointments flashed
through my mind. I reached the steep stairway to the platform and ran up,
two steps at a time. Blocking my path at the top was a heavy swinging door
with a large grimy window set into it; on the other side an old man in faded
work clothes was washing the glass with a spray bottle and rag. Out of the
middle of the grime he had just wiped a clean circle about a foot across,
through which, our noses inches apart, we now faced each other. Suddenly all the worry and hurry in which I had been caught up seemed to be
illuminated in the morning light breaking through the circle, and then to
drop away. It was as if the window were my clouded mind and the old man
with his rag had made a clear space for me to see, once again, that everything was light, everything was fine, and it always would be.

    Am I making too much of a simple encounter? (Did Dante?) I don't
know . . . maybe . . . yes and no. All I know is that the old man smiled
broadly, and in that moment I could have sworn he knew exactly what he
had done. Then he opened the door for me and stepped aside as the train
pulled into the station.

Prison
by Kevin Anderson[40]

      I'm doing too much.

      I'm doing too much
      time in the prison.

      I'm doing too much
      time in the prison
      of my self.

      I'm doing too much
      time in the prison
      of my self-
      elected busyness.

Don't Make Lists
by Dorothy Walters[41]

> Every day a new flower rises
> from your body's fresh soil.
> Don't go around looking
> for fallen petals
> in a fairy tale, when you've
> got the golden plant
> right here, now,
> shooting forth in light from your eyes,
> your awakening crown.
>
> Don't make lists, or explore ancient accounts.
> Forget everything you know
> and open.

Starting from Scratch
by Ingrid Wendt[42]

> To begin with, none of your neighbors began here.
> Everyone moved in years before you moved into
> a pattern you found yourself part of
> before you intended: flowers, fences,
> attention to the details your mother always took care of,
> duller than film on dishes it was always your job to wipe.
> Nobody spoke about courage.
>
> Nobody said you could choose this life.
> It happened, it didn't, the fact
> you could choose to remain would become
> what's yours to control: hours
> of sleeping and waking, meals, the home
> you need to go out in the world from.
> Neighborhood customs you know you can count on.
>
> Recipes, grapes exchanged for zucchini, the garden
> someone will know when to plant.
> The book you suggest. The pattern of limits
> no one has asked for, told over coffee, lives
> like yours you could have become
> starting from scratch. Each day
> the way you will live before what comes next.

FIVE

DISCERNING INTENTIONS

On one occasion when Jesus was going to the house of a leader of the Pharisees to eat a meal on the sabbath, they were watching him closely. Just then, in front of him, there was a man who had dropsy. And Jesus asked the lawyers and Pharisees, "Is it lawful to cure people on the Sabbath, or not?" But they were silent. So Jesus took him and healed him, and sent him away. Then he said to them, "If one of you has a child or an ox that has fallen into a well, will you not immediately pull it out on a sabbath day?" And they could not reply to this. (Luke 14:1–6)

Reflections
BY CAREN

Within the tiny, tidy confines of my mother's condo in Florida, Sabbath always ended at a time certain: Saturday, 6:15 p.m., regardless of when the sun actually set. For Mom the letter of Jewish law never determined the official close of her weekly refrain from life's routine occupations. Instead, her time of rest, reflection, and reconnection with self and God ended dutifully, yet lovingly, on a schedule yet to be published on any Jewish calendar.

Rather religiously, after walking to her Orthodox synagogue in the morning, sitting through services in the women's section lasting three or more hours, kibitzing at the shared meal afterward, and returning home to neither flick a light switch, answer or make a phone call, put pen to paper, render recipes into meals, nor do anything else "prohibited" on Shabbat, Mom would retreat to her screened porch. Years earlier she transformed the 8 x 10-foot room into a botanical garden. Plants—green, speckled yellow, red tinged, and some a-blooming with orchids and other tropical delights—filled the tile-floored sanctuary. It was here that she would sit for hours re-reading the weekly Torah portion, pondering the wisdom of Jewish sages, and murmuring favorite psalms to herself, her cat, Emily, and God.

Then at the aforementioned quarter hour, Mom would lay down her books or awaken from a doze and begin Havdalah, the prescribed close of Shabbat. Like the prayers and rites twenty-four hours earlier that served as Shabbat's overture, she conducted its finale over her kitchen table in a manner never rushed or lacking heart. At the end, she would kiss the binding of her prayer book reverently, set it back in its open slot on the bookshelf, move into the living room purposefully, and perform the last habitual ritual of the day. First, the settling into her favorite easy chair with Emily on her lap. Then, the picking up of the remote control. And lastly, the turning on of the televised ice-dancing competitions that began at 6:30.

"Mom, explain your take on Shabbat, " I said, to the petite author of an award-winning poem on the day of rest.

So she did during a Shabbat visit when shared family stories, reflections, and tears of laughter and sorrow made the hours pass like minutes. Predictably, about 6:15 that particular summer day, as the sun continued to shine with no signs of dusk or dark on the horizon and the clock ticked toward the time for ice skaters to dance flawlessly across the nearby screen, we stood together in prayer. Kisses on the prayer book binding and on my cheek, along with a tight hug, sealed the moment before Mom settled into the nearby easy chair she claimed as her own in my house. While looking at the serene smile on her face, I knew her take on Shabbat came from one who believed that God would approve. And it felt good.

Okay, so now let me back up.

I'd like to think that the word *adventure* best describes my mother's journey through the doorway that led her back to the faith of her ancestors. However, those who knew her in that chapter of her life would probably add others: steadfast, committed, loving, compelling, occasionally obsessive. A local Jewish newspaper that interviewed her about the path leading from her secular past to her commitment to become an observant Jew reported that one of her grandchildren was the stimulus for her conversion experience. "When my grandson began attending a Jewish elementary day school, I decided to enroll in a two-year Jewish mini-school for adults. I don't know what happened to me. I got caught up in it. I started to believe more and more . . . and I wanted to be a part of it," she confessed to the reporter and anyone else who asked.

During the second year of the program, my mother discovered that she could no longer eat lobster. "The food didn't want to go down and so I decided to keep kosher."

Doing so was, indeed, a proverbial labor of love that nurtured her newly planted beliefs. For example, on one visit I went out to her patio and found myself shouting back to the living room: "Why do you have your stainless knives and forks and spoons and a ladle and tongs sticking in these flowerpots like you were expecting them to send out new branches or sprout volunteers or become sterling silver?"

"It's has not been easy to become kosher again and keep meat and dairy dishes and two sets of eating utensils separate after all these years," she said. Her comment reminded me that before my parents were divorced my mother kept a strict kosher kitchen and even had a refrigerator for meat and another for dairy. But in the twenty-five years that had passed since my mother closed that shared kitchen and opened her own, she had been eating everything with anything. "When it comes to silverware, I keep accidentally using one with the other," she explained. "A meat spoon goes into a lovely potato soup made with cream; I grab a butter knife to cut a good Kosher hot dog, and a steak knife to cut butter. Instead of throwing them away, there's this process to make them kosher again. I'm a slow, slow learner. Some days I have more silverware than plants out here and I don't even throw dinner parties."

I never told her that planting silverware was lore, not law. She never asked. That's the way it was. When it came to being Jewish again for the first time, if the good deed felt right in her heart and the intention made sense in her head and together they filled her soul, she believed, wholeheartedly, that it was pleasing to God.

And thus her understanding of Shabbat. "I love Shabbat. It's the most beautiful day of the week," she said parentally. "I don't observe it just because God commands us to do that. I observe Shabbat because my week and even my life would feel incomplete without it. It helps me to heal the fragmented parts of myself and feel whole."

"But what about ending Shabbat so you can watch television?" I asked again.

"The law says we should love God with all our heart, mind, and soul. Caren, I'm an old lady who has shrunk a few inches in the last few years. If I could twirl and glide like those ice skaters to use my body, mind, and spirit to express my love of God at the end of Shabbat I would—I truly would. And in some ways I do when I watch that program. I see the skaters' beauty and grace and something in me joins them and feels more alive and whole and connected to God's love."

Wonderings and Wanderings

Before entering into this story about Jesus, describe in your words what is taking place in the exchange between Jesus and the Pharisees.

Now read the passages below from the Torah. List or underline verbs and phrases that specify what one should and should not do on the Sabbath.

> Remember the Sabbath day, and keep it holy. Six days you shall labor and do all your work. But the seventh day is a Sabbath to the LORD your God; you shall not do any work—you, your son or your daughter, your male or female slave, your livestock, or the alien resident in your towns. For in six days the LORD made heaven and earth, the sea, and all that is in them, but rested the seventh day; therefore the LORD blessed the Sabbath day and consecrated it. (Exodus 20:8–11)
>
> Six days you shall do your work, but on the seventh day you shall rest, so that your ox and your donkey may have relief, and your homeborn slave and the resident alien may be refreshed. Be attentive to all that I have said to you.
>
> But the seventh day is a Sabbath to the LORD your God; you shall not do any work—you, or your son or your daughter, or your male or female slave, or your ox or your donkey, or any of your livestock, or the resident alien in your towns, so that your male and female slave may rest as well as you. Remember that you were a slave in the land of Egypt, and the LORD your God brought you out from there with a mighty hand and an outstretched arm; therefore the LORD your God commanded you to keep the Sabbath day. (Exodus 23:12–14)

Offer reasons why the leader of the Pharisees would have asked Jesus to join him for a Shabbat meal?

As Jesus ventures forth, imagine that you are one of the Pharisees who, along with the lawyers, are watching him closely.

- Watching him for what?

Suddenly, a man with dropsy appears in front of Jesus. *Dropsy* is an archaic term for edema, an abnormal buildup of fluid between cells. Seeing this man, you make some assumptions about him based upon his appearance.

- Is there anything else you know about him?

According to the Gospel, this man never asks Jesus for anything. However, upon seeing the man, Jesus asks you, the other Pharisees, and the lawyers—all people grounded in Jewish law—a question about curing on the Sabbath.

- How do you explain your silence in response to Jesus' question about the Sabbath?

Describe your reaction to Jesus then taking the man, and when the man was healed, sending him on his way.

Write, in your own words, what you hear in the law and between the lines when Jesus speaks of pulling an ox or a child out of the well on the Sabbath.

- Again, when Jesus makes the comparison, no one says anything to him. Do you have unspoken thoughts and responses?

Explain differences between obeying the letter of the laws that govern our land and institutional religious practices and beliefs—and living into and out of the intent of those same laws.

- Who comes to mind when you think about those who know the law, respect the law, champion the law, and yet interpret and re-interpret the law?
  – Do particular thoughts, actions, or deeds stand out for you?
- Where in your daily life, psyche, and soul do you feel bound up by "authorities"?

Remember a time when you dared to make your own decisions over and against the conventional and established interpretations of laws, and commandments in your home, educational institution, workplace, religious community, neighborhood, or country.

- What prompted your choice?
- In retrospect, was it worth it?

Mirrors

If we are spiritual beings on a human path rather than human beings who may be on a spiritual path . . . then life is not only a journey but a pilgrimage or quest as well. When we experience sacred moments it often is not so much a matter of outer geography but of finding soulful places within ourselves.

—Jean Shinoda Bolen[43]

If God had wanted us to be robots, He would have provided us with all the answers beforehand and so deprived us of any opportunity for free-

dom of choice. But the moment God wanted us to be human beings and
have the Divine Image . . . God had to leave us a gray area where we are
able to shape our own world and life through our own free choice.

—Rabbi Daniel Tropper[44]

From *Long Life: Essays And Other Writings*
by Mary Oliver[45]

In the shapeliness of a life, habit plays its sovereign role. The religious literally wear it. Most people take action by habit in small things more often
than in important things, for it's the simple matters that get done readily,
while the more somber and interesting, taking more effort and being more
complex, often must wait for another day. Thus, we could improve ourselves quite well by habit, by its judicious assistance, but it's more likely
that habits rule us.

[I]f you have no ceremony, no habits, which may be opulent or may be
simple but are exact and rigorous and familiar, how can you reach toward
the actuality of faith, or even a moral life, except vaguely? The patterns of
our lives reveal us. Our habits measure us. Our battles with our habits
speak of dreams yet to become real. I would like to be like the fox, earnest
in devotion and humor both, or the brave, compliant pond shutting its
heavy door for the long winter. But, of yet have I reached that bright life
or that white happiness—not yet.

From *The Poisonwood Bible*
by Barbara Kingsolver[46]

If I could reach backward somehow to give Father just one gift, it would
be the simple human relief of knowing you've done wrong, and living
through it. Poor Father, who was just one of a million men who never did
catch on. He stamped me with a belief in justice, then drenched me in
culpability, and I wouldn't wish such torment even on a mosquito. But
that exacting, tyrannical God of his has left me for good. I don't quite know
how to name what crept in to take his place. Some kin to the passion of
Brother Fowles, I guess, who advised me to trust in Creation, which is
made fresh daily and doesn't suffer in translation. This God does not work
in especially mysterious ways. The sun here rises and sets at six exactly. A
caterpillar becomes a butterfly, a bird raises its brood in the forest, and a
greenheart tree will only grow from a greenheart seed. He brings drought
sometimes, followed by torrential rains, and if these things aren't always

what I had in mind, they aren't my punishment either. They're rewards, let's say, for the patience of a seed.

The sins of my fathers are not insignificant. But we keep moving on. As mother used to say, not a thing stands still but sticks in the mud. I move my hands by day, and by night, when my fever dreams come back and the river is miles below me, I stretch out over the water, making that endless crossing, reaching for balance. I long to wake up, and then I do. I wake up in love, and work my skin to darkness under the equatorial sun. I look at my four boys, who are the colors of silt, loam, dust, and clay, an infinite palette for children of their own, and I understand that time erases whiteness altogether.

Tin Ear
by Peter Schmitt[47]

> We stood at attention as she moved
> with a kind of Groucho shuffle
> down our line, her trained music
> teacher's ear passing by
> our ten- and eleven-year-old mouths
> open to some song now forgotten.
> And as she held her momentary
> pause in front of me, I peered
> from the corner of my eye
> to hers, and knew the truth
> I had suspected.
> In the following days,
> as certain of our peers
> disappeared at appointed hours
> for the Chorus, something in me
> was already closing shop.
> Indeed, to this day
> I still clam up
> for the national anthem
> in crowded stadiums, draw
> disapproving alumni stares
> as I smile the length of school songs,
> and even hum and clap
> through "Happy Birthday," creating
> a diversion—all lest I send

the collective pitch
careening headlong into dissonance.
It's only in the choice acoustics
of shower and sealed car
that I can finally give voice
to that heart deep within me
that is pure, tonally perfect, music.
But when the water stops running
and the radio's off, I can remember
that day in class,
when I knew for the first time
that mine would be a world of words
without melody, where refrain
means do not join,
where I'm ready to sing
in a key no one has ever heard.

What Is God
by An Anonymous Third Grader[48]

You should always go to church on Sunday because it makes God happy, and if there's anybody you want to make happy it's God. Don't skip church or do something you think will be more fun like going to the beach. This is wrong. Besides, the sun doesn't come out at the beach until noon anyway.

SIX

BECOMING WELL

On the way to Jerusalem Jesus was going through the region between Samaria and Galilee. As he entered a village, ten lepers approached him. Keeping their distance, they called out, saying, "Jesus, Master, have mercy on us!" When he saw them, he said to them, "Go and show yourselves to the priests." And as they went, they were made clean. Then one of them, when he saw that he was healed, he turned back, praising God with a loud voice. He prostrated himself at Jesus' feet and thanked him. And he was a Samaritan. Then Jesus asked, "Were not ten made clean? But the other nine, where are they? Was none of them found to return and give praise to God except this foreigner?" Then he said to him, "Get up and go on your way; your faith has made you well." (Luke 17:11–19)

Reflections
BY CAREN

In the mid 1980s the news came in hushed and guarded tones to the Jewish weekly paper where I worked as an editor. "Someone, son of so-and-so, died of AIDS in San Francisco," a colleague reported. Mere minutes passed before those of us with decision-making powers were called to meet behind a closed door.

This was a time in newsrooms nationwide when biblical-sounding words described AIDS: plague, scourge, curse, punishment, God's wrath, sinners. Terms such as *AIDS-related causes* had not yet become standard media catchphrases for a plethora of life-threatening illnesses jump-started by the mysterious, frightening, and opportunistic disease. Indeed, few had the right words to describe AIDS victims, although almost everyone had something to say about them.

"We can't put the actual cause of death in the paper," said the editor-in-chief as she began problem-solving. "His family will be humiliated. We can't talk publicly about the fact that this disease affects our community. People are in denial. People are scared. How should we deal with this?"

Solutions poured freely into a reservoir of brainstorming that flowed until an uncomfortable silence forced a decision. "He had cancer when he died," the publisher said. "The obituary will report, honestly, that he died of cancer."

During the pause that allowed the solution to the problem to compute, most heads bobbed yeses, accompanied by sighs of relief. However, a couple of us felt at odds, angry, and defeated about what would continue to be a cover-up—a blanket of half-truths about the human side of AIDS.

During those years, fears about catching AIDS, touching people with AIDS, and even admitting that you knew someone with AIDS settled into the heart of our nation—and our fears knew no boundaries. Political, religious, private, and public communities unabashedly condemned and marginalized gay, lesbian, and bisexual people, and openly proclaimed that God was punishing them. Rationalizations, justifications, excuses, and concocted stories abounded when someone outside the gay community became infected by transfusions, heterosexual men and women unfaithful to their partners, inadvertent needle sticks and pricks, infected blood spilled in a lab. Anything that sounded accidental and provided a fitting explanation.

In the wake of the fear, confusion, and embarrassment, parents, neighbors, and former friends kept AIDS patients at a distance by shunning and disowning them. Churches and synagogues closed their doors to the questions about AIDS begging their attention. Sometimes they even closed their doors to the people with the disease. Hospitals isolated the problem with new quarantine units and protective gear. To the world-at-large, those with AIDS were not only dying but in essence dead.

Statistics indicated that the problem would not just go away and public outcries mounted from religious institutions against "sinners" infected with the disease. Yet ever so slowly—some said miraculously—faithful saints emerged with healing hands willing to cross imprecise boundaries, challenge preconceptions about the disease, and support those dying from it.

Two of those healing hands belonged to my daughter, Jamie. Others belonged to the people in Ted's church in Toledo, Ohio. In the late 1980s

Jamie, who has an open and embracing heart that expands well beyond her chest, lived 150 miles south of us in Columbus—a typical Midwest metro area where the growing AIDS crisis made woeful nightly news. Talking with friends who had friends, relatives, or acquaintances with AIDS, Jamie decided to venture into a wilderness few had traveled and become what would later be known as a "buddy." Of course the job description for these early AIDS buddies came without an instruction manual, and so as medical professionals struggled to put together their template, Jamie opted to create her own. For her, the path was straightforward. She began walking it by reaching out to Mark, who had been cast out by his family. After work Jamie brought him home-cooked meals. On days off she provided companionship on their walks in the park or while watching television. And whenever they were together, she offered him one of the simplest and most precious gifts of all: latex glove-free hands and touches to an arm, cheek, hand, back, or feverish forehead.

In those days, Jamie's roadmap for healing was so unconventional that she and Mark became the subject of news reports. Some called her "brave" and "pioneering." She just called herself passionate about her beliefs that compassion was at the heart of healing even when there wasn't a cure and that this was what we are all called to do. It wasn't a choice, she declared. It was a mandate.

As Jamie worked hard to demythologize AIDS in Columbus, the people of St. Mark's in Toledo struggled to do the same in their corner of the state. It was 1989 and my job at the newspaper in another city was just a memory. Ted and I would be married in a few months. We felt excited about starting our life together in a new city, and he was especially eager to begin leading his new congregation, where a civil war lasting eight years had cut a swathe through the people in the pews and members of both factions had left. Indeed, on his first Sunday only forty, mostly elderly, people remained. Rows of empty seats in the neo-Gothic stone sanctuary with sixty-foot ceilings spoke of the decimation. However, within months of his first sermon, newcomers began arriving in response to a message that "We welcome all." A young couple showed up and asked to join and be married. A few who belonged long ago returned. Neighborhood residents who were church-hopping decided to stay. Some people came from afar, admitting they were gay and lesbian and that they'd never felt welcomed anywhere. And then, one Sunday, someone with telltale signs of AIDS walked in and up the aisle for Communion.

In response to the curiosity, questions, concerns, and complaints that followed the arrival of the stranger in their midst, Ted taught and preached and asked what it would mean to take seriously what Jesus took seriously. Established congregants answered by shaking their heads—some yes, some no. At first, when it came time to pass the peace or take Communion with "those people," many in the congregation who looked uncomfortable kept their distance. Some left for other churches. Others asked questions: "Why can't we take Communion out of individual paper cups?" "What if we only shake hands with people we know?" "What will we do if someone catches AIDS from this person?" "Why do we have to be the ones to let these people in? Why do *we* have to be the ones to show mercy?"

And then finally: "How do we begin to figure out what God really wants and then do something about it?"

Not long after, St. Mark's Toledo became the first church in a city of over five hundred churches to publicly invite people with AIDS, their families, and friends to worship. They also became the first place in Northwest Ohio to display four panels of the AIDS Memorial Quilt. Words spoken during the opening of the display in the narthex of the church were a rallying cry to look among and within to view all people in all corners of the kingdom of a loving and forgiving God. And in the years that followed, the people of St. Mark's did just that while praising God in word and deed.

Wonderings and Wanderings

About Samaritans

On the way to Jerusalem, Jesus was traveling between Samaria, a foreign land, and Galilee—home base. Samaria was the capital of the northern kingdom that dated back to the split of the united empire in the days following Solomon's reign. According to Biblical scholars, ten of the twelve tribes descended from Abraham, Isaac, and Jacob became a kingdom in the north called Israel. In the south, the two remaining tribes became the kingdom called Judah (later Judea). The Assyrians occupied and destroyed Israel in 722 BCE and afterward they moved part of the native population out and people from elsewhere in the Middle East in. These diverse inhabitants called themselves Samaritans. They practiced the Israelite religion and used their own version of the five books of Moses as their Bible. Instead of worshipping at the Temple in Jerusalem, they built their own version of the Temple on Mount Gerizim in the fourth century BCE. Scholars report that in Jesus' time the Samaritans and the Jews each claimed the same God, the same ancestry, and the same text. Like any religious rivals—Catholics and Protestants in various locations, or Sunni and Shi'ite—the two groups loathed each other.

About "leprosy"

What the Israelites considered to be a "leprous disease" is defined in the Torah (Leviticus 13) and includes a number of various skin ailments and sores. It also prescribes the behavior of one who has been deemed "leprous":

> The person who has the leprous disease shall wear torn clothes and let the hair of his head be disheveled; and he shall cover his upper lip and cry out, "Unclean, unclean." He shall remain unclean as long as he has the disease; he is unclean. He shall live alone; his dwelling shall be outside the camp. (Lev. 13:45–46)

However, in Jesus' time, Jews were no longer in a "camp" traveling with the Ark of the Covenant, and people with leprosy were no longer restricted to living alone and dwelling "outside the camp."

Look off into the distance and see the same people with leprosy that Jesus sees. Write down a list of words that describe your immediate impressions of them physically and figuratively.

Upon seeing Jesus, the ten call do not call out, "Unclean, unclean." Instead, they call out "Jesus, Master, have mercy on us!" In your own words, define "mercy" and in particular describe the "mercy" that the people with leprosy are asking for.

The text says, "he saw them." Rephrase what Jesus sees besides ten leprous men.

- Jesus tells the lepers to present themselves to the priests in accordance with Jewish law (Leviticus 14). "And as they went, they were made clean. Then one of them, when he saw that he was healed, he turned back, praising God with a loud voice." The Greek word for "made clean" is *katharizo*, meaning cleanse or purify or declare ritually acceptable. The Greek word for "healed" is *iaomai*, which means cured of disease or restored. What does this add to your reading?

  "[W]hen he saw that he was healed . . . he prostrated himself at Jesus' feet and thanked him. And he was a Samaritan." Only after the healing do we learn that the one who returns was the Samaritan—the foreigner—living in community with nine Jews suffering from the same physical condition. Considering the animosity between the Jews and the Samaritans in those days:

  – As a Samaritan, how might he have felt living among Jews?

– As a "leper," how might he have viewed his place in society?
– As a Samaritan "leper," how might he have viewed his relationship to the other "lepers" in his community?

When the Samaritan returns praising God, Jesus says, ". . . your faith has made you well." The Greek word for "made well" is *sozo* and is translated as save, deliver, preserve, cure, and make whole. Express in your own words the relationship between faith and healing in this story.

After telling the Samaritan that his faith has made him well, Jesus tells him to go.

• Go where? To do what? With whom?

Name the men and women in today's world who get labeled the way "lepers" were labeled in the time of Jesus.

• How do those labeled this way in today's world "keep their distance" either alone or in community?
• How do people in your world keep them at a distance?
• To whom are these people shouting, and what are the mercies they ask for?

Expand your perspective by casting people in the world today who get pejoratively labeled "lepers" and "Samaritans" in your own version of this story. Describe the plot, the players, and those who respond to cries for mercy.

Look in a mirror and within yourself, and name parts of you that either you or another may have consciously or unconsciously labeled "leper."

• Can you name ways in which people have kept their distance from you?
    – In what ways have you distanced yourself from this part of you?
• Do these parts of your body, mind, or spirit ever call out for "mercy"?
    – If so, what are they really asking you to do?
• Where must you go or what must you do for that part of you to feel cleansed, healed, and restored?
• How might praising God be a part of your healing and cleansing process?
• And for you, what is the meaning of a "faith" that might cause you to be made well?

Teach me to feel another's woe,
To hide the fault I see,
That mercy I to others show,
That mercy show to me.
  —Alexander Pope[49]

A faith that can be destroyed by suffering is not faith.
  —Richard Wurmbrand[50]

A sentinel angel sitting high in glory
Heard this shrill wail ring out from Purgatory:
"Have mercy, mighty angel, hear my story!"
  —John Hay[51]

To be merciful is to treat a person less harshly than, given certain rules, one has a right to treat that person.
  —Jeffrie Murphy[52]

The quality of mercy is not strain'd, It droppeth as the gentle rain from heaven upon the place beneath. It is twice blest, It blesseth him that gives, and him that takes.
  —William Shakespeare[53]

Doubt is the disease of this inquisitive, restless age. It is the price we pay for our advanced intelligence and civilization. It is the dim night of our resplendent day. But as the most beautiful light is born of darkness, so the faith which springs from conflict is often the strongest and the best.
  —Robert Turnbull[54]

The way to see by faith is to shut the eye of reason.
  —Benjamin Franklin[55]

That's the thing about faith. If you don't have it you can't understand it. And if you do, no explanation is necessary.
  —Major Kira Nerys, *Star Trek: Deep Space Nine*[56]

One Song
by Rumi[57]

> All religions, all this singing
> One Song.
> The differences are just
> Illusion and vanity.
> The Sun's light looks
> A little different on this wall than
> It does on that wall,
> And a lot different on this other one,
> But it's still one light.
>
> We have borrowed these clothes,
> These time and place personalities
> From a light,
> And when we praise,
> We're pouring them back in.

From "Instrument of Thy Peace"
by Alan Paton[58]

> O Lord,
> open my eyes that I may see the needs of others;
> open my ears that I may hear their cries;
> open my heart so that they need not be without succor;
>
> let me not be afraid to defend the weak because of the
> anger of the strong,
> nor afraid to defend the poor because of the
> anger of the rich.
> Show me where love and hope and faith are needed,
> and use me to bring them to those places.
>
> And so open my eyes and my ears
> that I may this coming day be able to do some work of
> peace for thee.
> Amen.

SEVEN

RESISTING NOT EVIL

You have heard that it was said, "An eye for an eye and a tooth for a tooth." But I say to you, "Do not resist an evildoer. But if anyone strikes you on the right cheek, turn the other also; and if anyone wants to sue you and take your coat, give your cloak as well; and if anyone forces you to go one mile, go also the second mile. Give to everyone who begs from you, and do not refuse anyone who wants to borrow from you." (Matthew 5:38–42)

Reflections
BY CAREN

In the 1950s, people in our Brooklyn, New York neighborhood who weren't Jewish were seasonally conspicuous. Porches framed by green and red lights were real give-a-ways in December. Of course, if you were black your differences weren't confined to holidays. Such was the case with our neighbor down the street and around the corner named Jackie Robinson.

Although I was too young to be one of the kids on the block who regularly got to root for the groundbreaking Brooklyn Dodgers first baseman from the stands at Ebbets Field, I was old enough to remember Jackie visiting us in the schoolyard at PS 244 and telling stories about his life. Years after his death in 1972, I heard yet another that drove home many of his words to us.

As that story goes, when given the opportunity to move from playing in the Negro League into the world of white baseball for the Brooklyn Dodgers, Robinson knew it could cost him his career. But crossing that daunting threshold would also be the fulfillment of his dreams. He decided to go for it, but not before Branch Rickey, the Dodgers' manager, made the rookie promise that he would never retaliate for insults thrown at him.

"Mr. Rickey, are you looking for a Negro who is afraid to fight back?" Robinson asked.

"I'm looking for a ballplayer with guts enough not to fight back," Rickey countered.

As predicted, each time Robinson stepped out of the dugout the crowds chucked angry racial slurs at him. As promised, Robinson fielded the harsh words but never tossed them back. Invariably, his ability to face their abuse further inflamed the spectators as well as opposing players who shouted, "Shoe-shine boy!" "Black S.O.B." and "Nigger!"

Enter Dodgers' captain Pee Wee Reese, a Southerner. He called time out and then walked straight to Robinson as the players on the opposite team and the crowds on both sides insulted his teammate. Without saying a word, Reese put his arm around Robinson's shoulders and stared into the crowd until, at last, the umpire shouted, "Play ball."

Historically, Benazir Bhutto, Mahatma Gandhi, Martin Luther King, Jesus, and long lists of other leaders and martyrs have, like Robinson, paved the way for our understanding of how a person can "resist not evildoers." But ordinary people going about their daily routines and tasks have become unlikely heroes, in the face of extraordinary events too. Oskar Schindler, who saved the lives of hundreds of Jews during the Shoa. Peace Mom Cindy Sheehan, who lost her son to the war in Iraq. Archbishop Oscar Arnulfo Romero, who practiced nonviolence in the face of guerilla warfare in San Salvador. Floyd Cochran, who devotes his life to countering the white supremacy movement.

I don't remember how I heard about Cochran back in the mid-1990s, but when I did I knew I had to track him down and invite him to Toledo to speak at Ted's church. He arrived one Saturday, refusing to accept an offer to stay at our home and registering instead under a pseudonym in a shabby motel five miles out of town. When we finally met, I looked at his thin bearded face and into the sunken dark eyes of a hunched, haunted, hungry, and hunted looking chain-smoking man.

We approached each other and silently shook hands. He spoke first: "I'm followed all the time by right-wing extremists. So I need to just take care of me and only me when I go places. It's not safe for you to let me stay at your house."

"We would have taken the risk," Ted said.

"No. You wouldn't want to do that," Cochran replied. "I never know when they're following me, but they always do. They have attempted to kill me. I try to fight them with words. But they're serious about fighting me with weapons."

As we drove to Ted's church to show Cochran where he would speak, teach, and preach to congregants, students, and people of all colors and religions, he told a story repeated many times throughout the weekend. He was a self-proclaimed "loser" who grew up in foster homes in New York State. Failure was his life-long norm: he failed to have a stable family, he failed to finish high school, he failed to keep jobs and friends, he failed in his marriage and at fatherhood. He failed every other "opportunity" that came his way. Every opportunity except one.

While serving time in an upstate New York jail for unnamed crimes, Cochran developed a voracious appetite for all things Nazi and consumed everything about Adolph Hitler and the Third Reich that he could find. "When I learned that the neo-Nazi Christian Identity church known as the Church of Jesus Christ Christian/Aryan Nations was teaching Hitler's ideology," he said, "I knew I had to join."

Once out of jail, Cochran headed for the Aryan Nations' former compound in Northern Idaho. "When that opportunity came and it was possible for me to make the leap from reader to warrior, I felt certain a higher destiny was calling me."

As a Nations recruit, Cochran got a uniform, a gun, and round-the-clock indoctrination. But none of those trappings meant as much as just hearing from his superiors that he mattered and could be powerful. "For the first time in my life, I was important."

After his initial indoctrination and training, Cochran became a guard. Not long after, the leadership maximized the obedient soldier's talents as a creative and compelling speaker by moving Cochran from guarding the perimeter to the Nations' inner circle. Within two years his grit transformed him from a "loser" into the Nations' chief recruiter, national spokesman, and fifth-ranking leader. "I taught that white people, and white people only, were the sons and daughters of God. I read the Bible and went to church regularly. I practiced a religion called Christian Identity, which believes people with different skin colors and religions must be exterminated. For the first time, everything in my life seemed to have purpose."

Crisscrossing the country, Cochran recruited college and high school students in the name of God, not Hitler. "We used 'wedge issues' such as welfare, crime, and abortion to rally the youths by promoting fear and hate. I wouldn't walk up to people and say, 'Hey, you want to become a Nazi, you want to join a hate group, you to want to worship Adolph Hitler?' When I came to your community, I didn't pull out the swastikas. I pulled out the Bible and used it to support and explain Christian Identity theology."

On the night in 1992 that Cochran returned to the Idaho compound to prepare for the Annual Hitler Youth Festival, he felt invincible. The Aryan Nations' leader, Rev. Richard Butler, had dubbed him "the next Goebbels," and Cochran knew he would be the chosen one when Butler stepped down. So when guards met him at the gate and took him aside to talk about a problem, he never suspected what followed. "They told me that my four-year-old son, who was born with a cleft palette, was a defect who had to be euthanized. My head started spinning and I felt like I was going to throw up. Just like all the people I hated, looked down on, and wanted to exterminate, my innocent son was being targeted. They wanted to kill him for something he had no control over." Cochran knew he had to leave forever. Once Butler knew, he gave Cochran five minutes to get out.

In the weeks that followed his "escape," Cochran lived in a tent while battling fear, guilt, and demons of mythological proportions. He also knew he now needed to do everything he could to first protect his son and then himself. Knowing how treacherous the turf he had yet to traverse would be, Cochran eventually connected with a preeminent organization in Atlanta that was working to combat racism, bigotry, and white supremacy. Once the Center for Democratic Renewal heard his story, they put him in touch with Leonard Zeskind, a progressive, nonmilitant, antifascist activist in Kansas.

"Zeskind contacted me and all he said was, 'Do you want to talk?' So we met and I talked while he listened. The whole time he never condemned me for my beliefs. He never attacked me or argued with me. He never asked for anything. I kept waiting for all that, but instead, when I finished telling him my stuff, he only asked if I had a place to live."

When Cochran said, "No," Zeskind took him into his home. "It was the first bed I had slept in for more than a month. He even let me stay long enough to get my head straight and begin to figure things out for me and my son. It baffled me. Why would a stranger do all that? And you want to know the craziest part of it all? Leonard Zeskind is Jewish."

Wonderings and Wanderings

This passage opens with Jesus saying: *"You have heard it said. . . . ."* When you hear such a phrase, what pops into your mind?

The oft-quoted commandment "an eye for an eye and a tooth for a tooth" is attributed to Moses. It appears in the books of Exodus, Deuteronomy, and Leviticus. Here is the Scripture in context:

Exodus 21:22–24:

When people who are fighting injure a pregnant woman so that there is a miscarriage, and yet no further harm follows, the one responsible shall be fined what the woman's husband demands, paying as much as the judges determine. If any harm follows, then you shall give life for life, eye for eye, tooth for tooth, hand for hand, foot for foot, burn for burn, wound for wound, stripe for stripe.

Leviticus 24:19–20:

Anyone who maims another shall suffer the same injury in return: fracture for fracture, eye for eye, tooth for tooth; the injury inflicted is the injury to be suffered.

Deuteronomy 19:15–21:

A single witness shall not suffice to convict a person of any crime or wrongdoing in connection with any offense that may be committed. Only on the evidence of two or three witnesses shall a charge be sustained. If a malicious witness comes forward to accuse someone of wrongdoing, then both parties to the dispute shall appear before the LORD, before the priests and the judges who are in office in those days, and the judges shall make a thorough inquiry. If the witness is a false witness, having testified falsely against another, then you shall do to the false witness just as the false witness had meant to do to the other. So you shall purge the evil from your midst. The rest shall hear and be afraid, and a crime such as this shall never again be committed among you. Show no pity: life for life, eye for eye, tooth for tooth, hand for hand, foot for foot.

- How have others—parents, clergy, teachers, media—interpreted this mandate for you?
  - Do you agree with them?
  - What more might you conclude, say, or add?

After quoting Moses, Jesus says, *"Do not resist an evildoer."*

- Who might the *"evildoers"* be in your own life and in the world around you?
- Describe the usual ways in which people like us physically, psychically, and spiritually resist and oppose evildoers overseas, in our communities, homes, and families.
- Normally, how do you defend against and resist evildoers in places far away and as close as your most intimate circles?
  - And those in your psyche and soul—what defenses do you use to resist their voices, urges, and threats?

In your own words, explain or outline the process and the implications of *not* resisting an evildoer.

Jesus says, *"But I say."*

- Does Jesus' use of the word *but* serve to clarify, expand, enhance, discount, or imply something overlooked or ignored about the intent of the ancient law?

Setting aside any preconceived notions you may have about this passage, think about the physical and psychic processes involved in turning the other cheek, giving your coat and cloak, and going the extra mile in the face of an evildoer. Think, too, of the potential outcomes.

- Does Jesus call for passivity or something else?
  - If something else, how would you elaborate on his words?

In your lifetime, who, when, where, and why did someone you respect and admire stand firm in the face of an evildoer and then turn the other cheek, give coat and cloak, or go the extra mile?

- And you?

Nonviolence seeks out conflict, elicits conflict, exacerbates conflict, in order to bring it out into the open and lance its poisonous sores. It is not idealistic or sentimental about evil; it does not coddle or cajole aggressors, but moves against perceived injustice proactively, with the same alacrity as the most hawkish militarist.
—Walter Wink[59]

Pacifism is not synonymous with passiveness. Instead, peace calls for courage in the face of evil and injustice, and bold, creative action.
—Karen L. Oberst[60]

If everyone lived by "an eye for an eye" and "a tooth for a tooth," the world would be blind and toothless.
—Tevye, in *Fiddler on the Roof*[61]

Act in such a way that you always treat humanity, whether in your own person or in the person of any other, never simply as a means, but always at the same time as an end.

—Immanuel Kant, from *Immanuel Kant* by Ruth Chadwick[62]

Stranger on the Bus

by Lawrence Kushner[63]

A light snow was falling and the streets were crowded with people. It was Munich in Nazi Germany. One of my rabbinic students, Shifra Penzias, told me her great-aunt, Sussie, had been riding a city bus home from work when SS storm troopers suddenly stopped the coach and began examining the identification papers of the passengers. Most were annoyed, but a few were terrified. Jews were being told to leave the bus and get into a truck around the corner.

My student's great-aunt watched from her seat in the rear as the soldiers systematically worked their way down the aisle. She began to tremble, tears streaming down her face. When the man next to her noticed that she was crying, he politely asked her why.

"I don't have the papers you have. I am a Jew. They're going to take me."

The man exploded with disgust. He began to curse and scream at her. "You stupid bitch," he roared. "I can't stand being near you!"

The SS men asked what all the yelling was about.

"Damn her," the man shouted angrily. "My wife has forgotten her papers again! I'm so fed up. She always does this!"

The soldiers laughed and moved on.

My student said that her great-aunt never saw the man again. She never even knew his name.

Rosa
by Rita Dove[64]

How she sat there,
the time right inside a place
so wrong it was ready.

That trim name with
its dream of a bench
to rest on. Her sensible coat.

Doing nothing was the doing:
the clean flame of her gaze
carved by a camera flash.

How she stood up
when they bent down to retrieve
her purse. That courtesy.

Revolutionary Dreams
by Nikki Giovanni[65]

i used to dream militant dreams
of taking
over america to show
these white folks how it should be
done
i used to dream radical dreams
of blowing everyone away with my perceptive powers
of correct analysis
i used to even think i'd be the one
to stop the riot and negotiate the peace
then i awoke and dug
that if i dreamed natural
dreams of being a natural
woman doing what a woman
does when she's natural
i would have a revolution

EIGHT

RECONCILING THE PAST

[Jesus said,] "You have heard that it was said to those of ancient times, 'You shall not murder'; and 'whoever murders shall be liable to judgment.' But I say to you that if you are angry with a brother or sister, you will be liable to judgment; and if you insult a brother or sister, you will be liable to the council; and if you say, 'You fool,' you will be liable to the hell of fire. So when you are offering your gift at the altar, if you remember that your brother or sister has something against you, leave your gift there before the altar and go; first be reconciled to your brother or sister, and then come and offer your gift."(Matthew 5:21–24)

Reflections
BY CAREN

Last night, for the hundredth or so time, I dreamed about being reconciled with my younger sister Deborah—Debby who hasn't spoken to me in eight years, which amounts to ninety-six months or 69,120 hours. During that time, my attempts to close the deep chasm created by my unknown and unconscious sin of commission or omission have been met with sheer silence.

Like many families who cannot move beyond differences and indifferences, my family rarely told stories about one another that had "happily ever after" endings. Instead, three D's—depression, deception, and division—seemed to be the customary outcome of our interactions. Such was *the* one that impacted my parents, Deborah, and me the most. I was nine years old.

A failed business partnership between my two childhood gods—daddy and my maternal grandfather—resulted in late night shouting matches peppered with words like "liar," "betrayal," "manipulation," "thief," "cheater," and "#$°!!@&$)@^!!" One round of mayhem always seeded others and each brutalized my mother as she stood bewildered in the middle. The night the militant warfare ended outside the legal battlefield still in the courts, my mother's parents and sister detonated a bomb that devastated her psyche and soul. They disowned her. And as the oldest grandchild who often bounded down four city blocks and up the two flights of stone steps to watch my Nana cook or to run to the nearby bakery for her Jewish rye, or to just luxuriate in the fact that I was the apple of my grandfather's only good eye (he was blind in the other), the realization that I, too, was existentially dead to these beloved people wreaked emotional havoc.

Time to heal passed in its own way and on its own schedule. Months after the cut-off, I held an unshakable belief in my father's version of the story. I reduced grieving the loss of my grandparents to reminders of the new rules concerning them. Now I could no longer mention their names, or climb those familiar steps, or expect my upcoming tenth birthday to be acknowledged, or anticipate Passover feasts when Grandpa and Daddy would recall escapes from their ancestors' physical and emotional bondage and the hope for freedom and new life in Jerusalem.

One day, news came that my grandfather was ill. "Stomach cancer," my father reported briefly in a tone that had nary a hint of concern or compassion. "No," he screamed at my mother, "You cannot contact them. If you do and I lose this lawsuit it will be your fault."

Maybe it was weeks, or perhaps months later, that an invitation arrived, filled with the anticipation and hope that accompanies most reunions. "It will be your grandfather's sixty-sixth birthday next week," my mother said in her most indifferent tone. "They want you and your sister to come over for a party."

"Are you going too, Mommy?"

"No, just you and Debby. Here's some money. Go buy a gift."

"What should I get?" I asked.

"Whatever you want."

With the precious dollars stuffed in my pocket, symbolizing more than anything money could buy, I set out for the neighborhood stores five blocks away. Walking purposefully with an occasional skip or two to propel me forward faster, I headed toward the bakery where I still bought rye bread for Mommy's corned beef and pastrami lunches and the newspaper stand with a soda fountain producing ten-cent egg creams with foam that rose above the top of the glass. Then marching onward I passed the store with barrels of lip-puckering half dill pickles and sauerkraut, crossed the trolley tracks, looked away from the non-kosher butcher who had pigs' feet in the window (Mommy declared those "disgusting"), and landed at my destination. This was not just a jewelry store but the best jewelry store ever—a mecca that always dazzled me when I walked by. And now it was the place—*the place* —where I could buy the perfect gift.

"So how can I help you?" the owner asked as I stood inside gazing at the trove surrounding me.

Staring at the tattoo on his arm that marked him a Holocaust survivor, I said, "I need the tie pin with the star in the window for my Grandpa's birthday. I hope I have enough money. It's very important. Really important. I can't tell you how important. This has to be the best gift I've ever given anyone."

"Show me vich one," he replied.

Outside, I pointed to the third tier of jewelry. "It's that blue one with a white star in the middle and the diamonds."

"Such an expensive vone that sapphire. Do you have enough for it?"

"I don't know," I said reaching into my pocket and pulling out the money, a pink rabbit's foot, and everything else I always stored there.

Looking at my stash, he asked about the gift. And so I told him. I told him about my father and grandfather, and my mother's tears and fears. I told him about losing my family to a war that wasn't my fault but made me feel guilty. And as tears came, I told him I was sorry. I didn't want to be a crybaby about it all, and I assured him I didn't really cry a lot, but I guess I got scared that when Grandpa stopped loving me he began hating me like he hated Mommy and Daddy. And now that my Nana asked me to come to Grandpa's party, because, as Mommy said, "he had cancer," and if I didn't bring the right present I might never see him again. "He always wears tie pins. I know this will be the most special one he's ever gotten," I said.

Reaching into the window he pulled out the pin and for the first time I saw the price tag. As my head fell in disappointment, I headed for the door while telling the jeweler I was sorry.

"Vat? You're not going to buy this? I should put it back?"

"I don't have that much money—even at home."

Looking perplexed, he turned the box over. "Oy vey. Vat is this doing in this box? Who put it there?" he said to some invisible other person in the store. "This perfect star sapphire and diamond tie pin should be $6.50."

My funds totaled the $5 my mother gave me and 30 cents I won from Gary Schulman flipping baseball cards. "I still don't have enough," I said sighing in despair.

"Vat, you haven't heard about credit? Your credit is good by me. You vill bring me the difference when you have it. Ve vill write it down on a note where you make a promise, and it vill be our secret."

Days later, with the beautifully wrapped box in a brown paper bag, Debby and I headed for Grandpa's. Inside were Nana, Aunt Fern and her son Dennis, my closest cousin and another victim of the war in our family. Nana hugged hard; Fern cautiously. Dennis ran over to say hi and it felt like we hadn't been apart for a day though it had been more than a year. "Grandpa's in the living room," said Nana. "Go."

I walked into the room hoping nothing had changed. So far it felt like nothing had. Debby followed. Grandpa was on the couch. He didn't look too sick. A little thinner—perhaps I didn't remember right.

"Come here," he said, "so I can see how you've grown." As we approached, I held out the gift.

"For me," he said while peeling away the wrapping paper. I watched and held a long, deep breath filled with pending delight. Then, as he opened the box, I let the air inside me explode and pushed my closed lips and clenched jaw into a smile.

"Oh," he said flatly. "Another tie pin just like the one I have. You know, Caren, Dennis always gives me the perfect gift. See what Dennis gave me. I'll have to exchange yours."

Minutes later all I could say was, "My stomach really hurts. . . . I think I'm going to throw up. I better go home."

I told my mother the same lie when she asked why we came home so soon. When I paid my debt to the jeweler and cried and expressed my anger, he listened as his head bobbed softly from side to side. One glance at his sad eyes assured me that he knew about the death of a dream.

I never saw my grandfather again. Years later, on Yom Kippur, when I could finally wrap my head around both sides of that family story, I found myself setting aside my anger, remembering him from a spacious place in my heart, and feeling reconciled to him. Who knows? Perhaps someday I will be reconciled *with* him.

Maybe I'm kidding myself when I say I am reconciled to Deborah. Once again, the thought of picking up a phone and trying to call reminds me that all my other efforts to reunite the walls of a deep chasm created by my unknown sin of commission or omission have been met with sheer silence—and another attempt will probably be futile. Maybe not. Remembering a gift that I left behind a long time ago, I find myself again praying to not only be reconciled to Deborah but with her and saying, "May a peace that passes all understanding enter our lives."

Wonderings and Wanderings

Jesus breaks this teaching into two parts. The first recalls the literal words of one of the Ten Commandments with Jesus' additional commentary. The second is a process for bringing one's gift to the altar.

Think about the word *murder* and see it as it appears in the headlines, in movies, on the nightly news, and possibly across town, around the corner, or even closer. Describe and explore its causes and effects literally and figuratively.

- How do words, judgments, conscious and unconscious actions and interactions with others cause people like us to feel as though a part of us has been killed?
- Where, when, and how have you experienced such a sudden and dramatic end to a relationship with another person or a part of your life?
  – And your way of reacting immediately or years later?

In the opening sentences of the passage, Jesus relates murder and anger toward one's brother or sister to judgment, councils, and even the fires of hell. Ponder the psychic implications of those liabilities.

Jesus refers to "the" altar that plays a central role in this passage. Enter into this phase of Jesus' teaching by recalling that before the destruction of the Second Temple in 70 CE, Jews took sacrificial gifts such as the fruits of their harvests to the Temple in Jerusalem. If an animal was to be sacrificed, they purchased it upon arriving in Jerusalem. The altar in the Temple was restricted to the Temple priests, who made the offerings. Not all sacrifices related to "moral sins." Many were thanksgiving offerings, or offerings regarding ritual purity (such as the offering Mary and Joseph make in Luke's gospel).

Revisit an encounter with an altar that you visited for a specific reason.

- What hopes, beliefs, or expectations went with you that you felt you could not experience another way?
- When, if ever, have you taken a gift with you to place on an altar?
  – Why?

In speaking of one's journey to placing a gift at the altar, Jesus directs your attention to "something" that a brother or sister may have against you. Name "somethings" that others called "brothers" and "sisters" may have against us.

- When have you known one of them to harbor one or more of those "somethings" toward you?
  – And your response to and feelings about the other's position?
- What, for you, did it mean or could it mean to be reconciled *to* that person?
- What, for you, did it mean or could it mean to be reconciled *with* that person?

Imagine yourself as the prime player in this teaching. Picture an altar you have visited or take time to create one of your own on a table or rug or corner of a room, or in a garden, under a tree, or somewhere else that feels appropriate. Select an item that has a special meaning to represent "your gift," or draw or make one from clay or found objects. Before moving toward the altar with this gift in hand, reread Jesus' teaching and specific directions for approaching the altar. Then actually follow his instructions or create a collage or timeline describing it. On the way remember, leave your gift, be reconciled to your "brother" or "sister," and finally return to make your offering. Once the offering is made, write about the journey.

- Is there something that comes from not leaving the gift first that could not happen in any other way?

Mirrors

Love thy neighbor as thyself: Do not do to others what thou wouldst not wish be done to thyself: Forgive injuries. Forgive thy enemy, be reconciled to him, give him assistance, invoke God in his behalf.
    —Confucius[66]

How much more grievous are the consequences of anger than the causes of it.
    —Marcus Aurelius[67]

I am part and parcel of the whole and I cannot find God apart from the rest of humanity.
    —Mahatma Gandhi[68]

For transgressions between a man and his fellow man, the Day of Atonement does not atone unless he has first reconciled his fellow man.
    —Mishnah[69]

From *The Book of Jewish Values*
by Joseph Telushkin[70]

The great rabbinic sage Rabbi Israel Salanter (1819–1883) was once spending the night at a shoemaker's home. Late at night, Salanter saw the man still working by the light of a flickering almost extinguished candle.

Rabbi Salanter went over to the man: "Look how late it is; your candle is about to go out. Why are you still working?"

The shoemaker, undeterred by the rabbi's words, replied, "As long as the candle is burning, it is still possible to mend."

For weeks afterward, Rabbi Salanter was heard repeating the shoemaker's words: "As long as the candle is burning, it is still possible to mend."

"Flood: Years of Solitude"
by Dionisio Martínez[71]

> The mime troupe is in town again. They want to reconstruct us
> bit by bit.
> This is where the house went up in flames.
> This is how we walked away, trying to salvage nothing.
> That's us, building our separate houses in the aftermath.
> There were ashes to be swept away, years of debris, pages and
> pages of unresolved music.
> Here we are, looking out of our respective windows at the space
> between us.
> Of all the illusions, forgetting is the most dangerous.

First Marriage
by Liam Rector

> I made it cross country
> In a little under three days.
> The engine blew out
>
> About a hundred miles north
> Of San Francisco, where I'd
> Hoped to start living again
>
> With a woman I'd abandoned
> Only a few months before.
> The reasons I'd left her were

Wincingly obvious
Soon as I got back
To her, and it didn't take long

Before I again left her.
In a few weeks I'd meet
The woman who became

My first wife, the one
With whom I spent
Almost the entirety

Of my twenties. It took
About twenty years
Getting over her, after

We divorced at thirty.
Broke then, I took
A bus cross-country

And was back in the East
By Christmas, thinking it
Would take three years maybe

To put this one behind me.
But getting over her
Happened as we were

Both in our third marriages,
Both then with children,
Heading for our fifties.

She came cross-country
To tend to me when I had
Cancer, with a 20% chance

Of recovery. The recovery
From all she had been to me,
Me abiding with her as long

As I did, took place finally
When we, her sitting on my bed
And me lying in it, held hands

And watched ourselves watching
TV, something we'd never quite
Been able to do comfortably

All those years ago. So many
Things turn this way over time,
So much tenderness and memory,

Problems not to be solved
But lived, and I resolved
Right then to start living

Only in this kind of time.
Cancer gave this to me: being
Able to sit, comfortably, to get

Over her finally, and to
Get on with the fight to live while
Staying ready to die daily.

"First Marriage" by Liam Rector, from The Executive Director of The Fallen World. © The University of Chicago Press, 2006.

Seen
by Mark Wunderlich[72]

In your field of vision, there is a place where no image is fixed,
where injury carved its cave of nothing,
gathered blackness around a splinter's wooden slip.
One eye, you say, scans the world.
The other examines the self's invisible wanting.
In that equation, I believe myself to be
the point connecting one destination to another,
somewhere you paused to draw lines to the next warm station.
I emit no light, no heat
but gather, in cupped hands, what fell to the ground
when limbs were shaken by your grasping wind.

NINE

NEEDING HELP

And just then some people were carrying a paralyzed man lying on a bed. When Jesus saw their faith, he said to the paralytic, "Take heart, son; your sins are forgiven." Then some of the scribes said to themselves, "This man is blaspheming." But Jesus, perceiving their thoughts, said, "Why do you think evil in your hearts? For which is easier, to say, 'Your sins are forgiven,' or to say, 'Stand up and walk'? But so that you may know that the Son of Man has authority on earth to forgive sins"—he then said to the paralytic—"Stand up, take your bed and go to your home." And he stood up and went to his home. When the crowds saw it, they were filled with awe, and they glorified God, who had given such authority to human beings. (Matthew 9:2–8)

Reflections
BY TED

My brother, David, lifted one front wheel and my sister Jane the other as I pushed Mom's wheelchair along the wooded path. The unwieldy rental unit was difficult to maneuver on the soft dirt trail veined with gnarled tree roots and peppered with the points of deep gray rocks. My sister Susan, crippled by polio as an infant and now suffering from post-polio syndrome, limped alongside carrying an extra oxygen tank, and my wife, Caren, pulled fallen branches to the side. Finally reaching the St. Francis of Assisi outdoor chapel and the memorial garden at Kanuga, an Episcopal conference center, we stood silently as Mom looked around. Mountain laurels and rhododendrons surrounded the simple split-log pews and maple, ash, locust, and oak trees created a lush canopy. A small stream flowed in front of a stone altar providing the natural music of water gently rushing over boulders. "Yes," she said as if answering her own question, "This is where I would like my ashes and your father's to be buried." As we turned to maneuver closer to the memorial garden Mom spotted a plaque with a short list of names. "Look! Bennett Sims is buried here. Your father and I will be among friends." Mom's delight and sweet contagious chuckle broke the tension of not knowing what to expect.

In their youth Susan, David, and Jane spent many summers at Camp Kanuga and they now lived nearby, drawn back to the mountains of western North Carolina by warmhearted memories. In the early 1970s my father, Ed, served as the chairman of the Kanuga board of directors. And thirty-six years earlier, while attending a conference just steps away from the memorial garden, I made the choice to abandon a doctoral program in mathematics and enter seminary instead. Now, on the verge of retiring from parish ministry, I stood on this hallowed ground, helping Mom tie up loose ends.

Just days before we began putting one more piece of Mom's healing journey in place—the tough piece that dealt with end-of-life issues and plans for celebrating her life at her funeral. Chronic emphysema, diabetes, high blood pressure, gastro-intestinal inflammation, and bad knees debilitated Mom's body. She was tethered to a 50-foot oxygen hose when she was at home, and leashed to portable bottles of oxygen whenever she journeyed out. Her prescribed medications, including morphine, insulin, antibiotics, blood thinners, and reflux inhibitors plus nineteen others, were doled out three times a day. Periodic cortisone shots relieved the pain in her knees, and fresh bandages and ointments soothed a persistent infected bedsore on her ankle.

During the winter of 2007, she battled pneumonia three times, and with each hospitalization she became progressively weaker, dispirited, and more bound to her bed. Upon returning home from the last hospital stay she exclaimed, "I'd rather die at home right now with my family close by than have a bunch of strangers taking care of me in the hospital."

"What can I do?" I asked.

"Help me. Help me figure this out, Ted," she answered softly as tears filled her eyes.

Although I never balked when it came time to counsel parishioners on end-of-life issues, her words, "Help me," followed and haunted me everywhere. I found myself avoiding the conversation and even, at times, resenting having to have it. Whenever Jane brought it up, I changed the subject. "Stop it!" I finally told myself. "Face it, Ted. Mom isn't the only one who needs help—you do, too." It took a while, but that spring Susan, David, Jane, and I, with the help of a guide book called *Five Wishes*, finally listened to Mom detail her death: the way she wanted to die, the way she didn't want to die, and what she wanted her funeral to be like. "I'm not afraid to die, because it means I'm going to see Ed again and I can't wait. It's the thought of how I die that really frightens me. I don't want to be gasping for breath," she said. "When I gasp for breath it feels like I'm suffocating and drowning and it is very scary. And most of all I want to be surrounded by my family."

As we continued to use the *Five Wishes* as a roadmap to guide us on Mom's journey to express her concerns and fears about dying, we crossed terrain leading to healthcare proxies, Do Not Resuscitate (DNR) orders, last will and testament decisions, hospice care, funeral hymns, and even what we might serve at the reception following the service. At the mention of food, Mom laughed and we took a lengthy detour. One of her favorite rituals was planning meals for the parade of people she invited for dinner several nights a week. "There must be plenty of good food for everyone." We assured her there would be and with that wish in place we hugged, finished sniffling, and began planning the menu.

Within a week of that discussion, Mom's pneumonia flared up. When she told her doctor about the *Five Wishes* and refused to go to the hospital he asked, "Millie, are you ready to begin a home hospice program? You are in end-stage emphysema and an infection such as this could result in your death. Hospice will control your discomfort and help relieve your anxiety—but are you sure that's what you want?" With a sigh of relief, Mom answered, "Yes."

A day later a hospice doctor, a nurse, and a chaplain visited her and applied balms to heal her body, mind, and soul. And they did. Now free of the paralysis caused by her fears of how, when, and where she would die, Mom once again embraced life with a wide smile that matched her open arms.

Morning and night, extended family, friends, neighbors, and even strangers from down the street and around the world visited often. Every trip outside became an adventure, whether to see a doctor, "walk" in a nearby sculpture garden, paint watercolors in a riverside park, stroll the aisles of a kitchen gadget store, try on shoes at the discount emporium, or search for "whatever" at—of all places—Sam's Club. At times we had to carry her to her destinations, but most of the time her joyous spirit carried us.

Early one fall morning Jane called. "The hospice nurse says it can go either way. I think you need to get here as soon as you can." While we were driving on I-95 my cell phone rang. Tears clouded my eyes as I got the news: "Ted, Mom died—just as she wanted to."

On the eighth anniversary of Pop's death, Mom died on fluffed up pillows in her own comfortable, quilt-covered bed, surrounded by family and friends and her hospice physician. Minutes before she closed her eyes, she began puckering her lips. "Who are you kissing?" Susan asked.

"It's your father. It's Ed. He's kissing me!" They were Mom's last words.

Just as Mom and her helpers planned, my parents' ashes were buried in the memorial garden. It was a gorgeous autumn day with the mid-afternoon sunlight filtering through the trees of gold, orange, and red. Mourners came from each coast and beyond. Grandchildren read comforting words from Scripture, and a bluegrass band provided the lingering music for her favorite hymns. Ashes were placed on the stone altar in urns that David, a potter, had made especially for this day. As we all sang "Love Lifted Me," we reverently carried the urns the few steps to the garden, listened to prayers of commendation, and watched as the ashes were poured into the ground and Mom's journey to be healed ended.

Wonderings and Wanderings

"And just then some people were carrying a paralyzed man lying on a bed." Close your eyes and look at this scene. Describe the paralyzed man's face, body, and clothes as he lies on the bed others carry.

- Who are the people who carry his bed and how do they look?
  Listen in on the conversation between those who help carry the bed, and the conversations they have with the paralyzed man.
- What are they saying to each other?

Consider the possible causes of paralysis for a person in the time of Jesus.

- How would such paralysis limit someone?
- How might that person be treated by family members, friends, neighbors, and strangers?

"When Jesus saw their faith . . ."

- What might the paralyzed man and/or his friends have done or said that Jesus would label as "faith?"

In the world around us people like you and me suffer from physical, emotional, and spiritual paralysis.

- What forces, from outside or from within, may contribute to their inability to function, impair their ability to act on their own behalf, or render them powerless?

In what areas of your life might you be paralyzed?

- How have you been limited by this inability to fully function?
- What physical, emotional, or spiritual trauma or dis-ease may have contributed to your paralysis?

"Take heart, son; your sins are forgiven." The root of the word *sin* comes from the Greek *hamartia*, which is an archery term meaning "falling short of or missing the mark."

- What might Jesus imply about the relationship between "sin" and paralysis?
- Past or present—what are the "marks" that you fall short of, or miss entirely, that you or others call "sins"?
- How might your "falling short of or actually missing the mark" be related to your paralysis?
- What has to happen for you to believe you are forgiven?
- Where might you have to go, or what might you have to do?
- Upon believing you have received forgiveness of those sins, what might heal in your life?

Name those in your life who might show up, or those whom you might call upon, to help you get to a place where you believe that your sins are forgiven and you can experience healing.

"When the crowds saw it, they were filled with awe, and they glorified God, who had given such authority to human beings."

- To what does this "authority" refer? The power to forgive sins? To heal? Both? Something else?
- To which "human beings" did God give this "authority"? To Jesus? To the paralytic? To his helpers? To the crowds? To everyone?
- If God has given "such authority to human beings" and that includes you, what can you do with it?

Mirrors

The wish for healing has ever been the half of health.
—Seneca[73]

Help me if you can, I'm feeling down
And I do appreciate you being round.
Help me get my feet back on the ground,
Won't you please, please help me.
    —The Beatles, from *Help*[74]

A friend is the first person who comes in when the whole world has gone out.
    —Anonymous[75]

There are four essential qualities of a healer: trust, faith, love and humility.
    —Elisabeth Kübler-Ross[76]

Perfect action is called that which is *obligatory*, free from attachment,
performed without desire or loathing, by one who does not seek the fruits
thereof.
    —*Bhagavad Gita*[77]

One bird, if there is only one,
dies in the night
by Marge Piercy[78]

> I dropped my spoon into my yogurt
> at the crack of bird against window.
> I ran in sneakers into the snow.
>
> Often their spleens rupture
> or their necks break. This one
> was tiny, stunned. The wind
> had fangs. Ice formed in my
> lungs as I picked it up.
> I put on my coat over it and walked.
>
> It woke up slowly, turning to stare.
> It clutched my finger by reflex
> after an hour. Nearby I could hear
>
> the sheer cries of its partners,
> little panes of ice breaking.
> I identified it at leisure, bird
>
> in my hand, Peterson's open.
> A golden crowned kinglet, so those cries
> were stitches that bound them together,

birds the size of a hen's egg
who must clutch each other all night
to survive winters, so they call

all day, where are you? Here
I am, here. Finally it beat its wings
panicstricken after two intimate hours.

How often I feel I need a certain
number of companions or possible allies
to survive, say passing through Utah

or South Carolina. I count women
in a crowd, guess at Jews, feminists,
lefties, writers, all those we count

as someone who might watch our backside
so it won't fall off, who might
warm us through a lethal night's freeze.

From *Help*
by Garret Keizer[79]

The headline in the *Caledonian Record*, which circulates in every nook of
Caledonia County, to Groton and to West Groton, to Victory and the edge
of Lunenburg and far beyond, reads, "Dr. (Lloyd) Thompson Publicly
Reprimanded." This is an action taken by the Vermont State Medical Practice Board. In the photograph, Thompson stands at a podium gazing rather
forlornly at something we cannot see. Perhaps he is listening to the repri-
mand. I wonder if he is thinking about his own death. He is dressed as he
might choose to be buried. He is wearing a tweed jacket and a bow tie.

In a stipulation filed Wednesday, Thompson admitted it was wrong for him
to have administered the drug Norcuron to an 85-year-old patient last
August. Norcuron is a drug that causes muscle paralysis.

Thompson had been treating the patient for 20 years. In August her condition deteriorated and when she suffered respiratory failure she was placed
on a ventilator while at Northeastern Vermont Regional Hospital. Two years
earlier she had signed a durable will which stated she did not want to be
placed on any artificial life support systems but only wanted to receive care
to relieve pain and maintain her dignity.

Attempts to take her off the ventilator resulted in great stress, with the
woman experiencing a feeling of suffocation and panic. Her family was in
the hospital room and shared this distress.

It was apparent that the woman was dying. In his statement to the board, Thompson said he wanted to make that happen as comfortably as possible. . . .

In his statement Thompson said he decided to use Norcuron because he was afraid the patient would awake and suffer just before death. He was also concerned about the family who would see this and hoped to spare them emotional pain. . . .

He said he cared for this patient for many years. "She was my friend."

Diagnosis
by Marcia Lee Anderson[80]

> We multiply diseases for delight,
> invent a shameful want, a horrid doubt,
> luxuriate in license, feed on night,
> make inward bedlam—and will not
> come out
>
> Why should we? Stripped of subtle
> complication,
> who could regard the sun except with fear?
> This is our shelter against contemplation,
> our only refuge from the plain and clear.
>
> Who would crawl out from under
> the obscure
> to stand defenseless in the sunny air?
> No terror of obliquity so sure
> as the most shining terror of despair
> to know how simple is our deepest need,
> how sharp, and how impossible to feed.

Waking
by David Whyte[81]

> Get up from your bed,
> get out from your house,
> follow the path you know so well,
> so well that you now see nothing
> and hear nothing
> unless something can cry loudly to you,
> and for you it seems

even then
no cry is louder than yours
and in your own darkness
cries have gone unheard
as long as you can remember.

These are hard paths we tread
but they are green
and lined with leaf mould
and we must love their contours
as we love the body branching
with its veins and tunnels of dark earth.

I know that sometimes
your body is hard like a stone
on a path that storms break over,
embedded deeply
into that something that you think is you,
and you will not move
while the voice all around
tears the air
and fills the sky with jagged light.

But sometimes unawares
those sounds seem to descend
as if kneeling down into you
and you listen strangely caught
as the terrible voice moving closer
halts,
and in the silence
now arriving
whispers

Get up, I depend
on you utterly.
Everything you need
you had
the moment before
you were born.

TEN

BEING POOR

Then [Jesus] began to speak, and taught them, saying:
"Blessed are the poor in spirit, for theirs is the kingdom of heaven.
"Blessed are those who mourn, for they will be comforted.
"Blessed are the meek, for they will inherit the earth.
"Blessed are those who hunger and thirst for righteousness,
for they will be filled.
"Blessed are the merciful, for they will receive mercy.
"Blessed are the pure in heart, for they will see God.
"Blessed are the peacemakers, for they will be called children
of God.
"Blessed are those who are persecuted for righteousness' sake,
for theirs is the kingdom of heaven.
"Blessed are you when people revile you and persecute you and
utter all kinds of evil against you falsely on my account.
"Rejoice and be glad, for your reward is great in heaven, for in the
same way they persecuted the prophets who were before you."
(Matthew 5:2–12)

Then he looked up at his disciples and said:
"Blessed are you who are poor, for yours is the kingdom of God.
"Blessed are you who are hungry now, for you will be filled.
"Blessed are you who weep now, for you will laugh.
"Blessed are you when people hate you, and when they exclude
you, revile you, and defame you on account of the Son of Man.
"Rejoice in that day and leap for joy, for surely your reward is great
in heaven; for that is what their ancestors did to the prophets."
(Luke 6:20–23)

Reflections
BY TED

"I'm dying of AIDS," Tam said. "The doctor says that I might make it to Christmas, but I'm not so sure, so I want to arrange for my funeral now. Although I'm not a member of St. Mark's I was hoping I could have it here . . . and I don't want to hide the AIDS thing."

Stunned, I replied, "Of course we'll do a service here. I'm honored that you've come to us." Tam continued as though I hadn't said anything and he had to get everything out in one breath. "All of my friends who've died of AIDS had wakes at a funeral home, or words just said at a grave," he went on. "I don't want that. I loved my church when I was a kid, but now they've turned their back on me. My church has real problems with gay people. It doesn't make any difference that my parents worshipped there. I grew up there, played with their kids, ate in their homes, prayed with them every Sunday, and everything else. I was even confirmed. But when they found out I was gay they acted as if I were contagious . . . and they don't even know about the AIDS. I'm pissed, Ted. I'm pissed about my church . . . and I'm really pissed about AIDS. But I don't want to leave this world feeling that way, so I was hoping that I could have a church service. It would be like a kind of blessing."

Tam was well known in the neighborhood as a musician, actor, mime, and owner of a bed and breakfast just a few blocks from St. Mark's. He had been to a number of events and meetings at the church, and I had been to a couple of parties at his gorgeous Queen Anne-style Mansion View Inn. But when he walked into my office I hardly recognized him. His clothes hung off his body, his thin and scraggly hair framed his dark sunken eyes, and his face was dotted with red sores.

"I really don't know what goes on to make all this happen, but I have some ideas . . . and I hope they aren't too outrageous," Tam said as his lips formed the slightest smile.

"We'll work together on this," I answered.

When I finished talking about the traditional ideas for music and readings at a funeral service Tam looked studious as he told me what he wanted. Then, just when I thought we were getting close to a final plan his faint smile reappeared. "And maybe a couple of dancers, or even a scene from a play?" he asked.

"Why not?" I replied. "Tam, you also said something about wanting a blessing. What would that look or feel like? What would make this funeral a 'blessing' for you?"

"Tough question. All I know is that it won't be just the words you showed me in the prayer book. I've had too many empty blessings made up of nothing but words. I guess it would feel like a blessing if I knew I left something good behind me in this life, and that the people I love and care about—and maybe even people I don't know—could act on it." He paused, and I waited. "Ted, people are shocked and afraid of me when they find out I have AIDS. Just look at me. They go out of their way to avoid being near me. Even some members of my family won't touch me let alone give me a hug. And I know it's true for my friends with AIDS," he said as his eyes welled up with tears. Catching himself before they spilled over, he turned them off and added, "That's the part that pisses me off more than anything else. But I can't go on feeling that way. I don't want to die pissed. It has to change."

That meeting marked the first of many. Several times we met in my office to work out the details of the service and say healing prayers for his mind and spirit, and other times we sat in a nearby park. However, as the weeks passed and Tam's weight dropped to ninety-five pounds, he began walking awkwardly with a cane. And then one day, when he called to say he could no longer walk, I began going to his bedside at the Mansion View Inn. As we continued amending and fine-tuning his plans, the conversation often turned to stories about his childhood, love of theater, and involvement in the renewal of the Old West End neighborhood. "Did you know that I own the three houses behind St. Mark's?" he asked during one of those visits.

I knew the houses well and became angry whenever I looked out my second floor office window and saw rats running in the narrow alley that separated the church and Tam's rundown Victorian era homes. From the parish hall, I could almost touch Tam's dilapidated carriage house sitting behind them. Of all the buildings, this large anachronistic urban barn was the worst eyesore. Over years of neglect, it became a favorite hangout for heroin addicts and homeless men who built fires on the dirt floor to keep warm on cold nights. Without knowing who the owner was or taking time to find out, I complained regularly to city agencies about the condition of the houses, and called the police whenever a fight broke out or I noticed someone dealing drugs.

"No, I didn't know you were the owner. I always thought of you as a gentleman innkeeper, not a slum landlord," I said sarcastically.

"That offends me," Tam said defensively. "Just look at the pictures in that box on my dresser. Once they were beautiful houses, but I haven't been able to keep up with them for a long time. Why don't you get the church to buy them?"

I apologized and mulled his suggestion. "We're a church, not a property management company," I said minutes later.

"I'm serious," Tam countered, "I would sell the properties to St. Mark's for what I owe on them and that way you could protect your back door."

Tam died two months later. His mime troupe, dancers, and a Dixieland jazz band led a horse drawn glass paneled white hearse with gleaming brass trim through the streets of his beloved Old West End neighborhood and made his funeral everything he had hoped it would be. Before the service ended more than one hundred mourners surrounding his casket placed their hands on the polished wood or on the person next to them knowing it would not be the last time that I, and many others, blessed Tam.

The following year the people of St. Mark's agreed to purchase the three houses from Tam's estate—motivated by a desire to "protect its back door." However, in the years that followed we gradually discovered that Tam's desire to be blessed and be a blessing would lead us in ways we never imagined. Volunteers and professionals painted, plastered, re-roofed, re-plumbed, re-wired, to renovate the houses into ten apartments that a social service agency leased to homeless families who were enrolled in programs to help make them self-sufficient. St. Mark's also acquired an adjacent and abandoned nursing home. It, too, was refurbished and the social service agency moved in and established a food pantry, a clothing distribution site for women seeking employment, and a voice mail service for the homeless to be in touch with counselors and potential employers. A charter school for elementary school underachievers leased the remaining space. A small plot of land in the midst of the buildings became a community vegetable garden where the church school children and their new neighbors planted beans and squash and greens and tomatoes. Collectively, the site—now named St. Mark's Ministries—became the largest social service location in Toledo.

Along the way the project faced a number of hurdles, yet even these challenges transformed themselves into opportunities. "I'm really angry," I said to Mary Clare, the director of a community development corporation that had its office in the church. "We've been renovating these buildings for two years and now the Historic District Commission won't let us tear down the carriage house. They say it has 'architectural significance.' Everyone knows it's nothing but a decaying firetrap, and it detracts from all the work we've done with the rest of St. Mark's Ministries."

"Have you thought about using it for more housing?" Mary Clare suggested. "I'm sure that we could find grant money to make that happen," she added confidently. Within days, Mary Clare, known city-wide as a change agent able to unravel tangled masses of bureaucratic red tape, called a meeting of leaders from her organization, St. Mark's, the local AIDS support services, and city housing officials. Soon after, a grant proposal was mailed to the federal Housing and Urban Development agency, and a year later, with HUD funding and additional grants from the Episcopal Church and a local foundation, we completed construction of three apartments inside the shell of the carriage house. The vision to use them to house homeless persons living with HIV/AIDS became a reality. The sign over the door read "Tam's House."

The dedication of the final phase of the ministry campus was a blessed event with dignitaries, church leaders, parishioners, and St. Mark's new next-door neighbors praying and celebrating. It concluded with a prayer of House Blessing from the Book of Occasional Services:

> Visit, O blessed Lord, this home with the gladness of your presence. Bless all who live here with the gift of your love; and grant that they may manifest your love to all whose lives they touch. May they grow in grace and in the knowledge and love of you; guide, comfort, and strengthen them; and preserve them in peace. . . .

Before the festivities ended, I headed back to my office and passed by the community garden. A car stopped, and a woman called to me. I turned around to see who it was. "Pastor, is it okay for us to pick some of those vegetables?" she said. "It's the end of the month. We don't have food at home, and I got all these mouths to feed."

"Sure," I said. "Go right ahead. That's what this garden is for. Pick whatever you need."

"Oh, praise God!" she exclaimed. "Thank you, and thanks to whoever planted these seeds. This is a real blessing."

Wonderings and Wanderings

See yourself as a poor, hungry, or despairing person who is in the crowd listening to Jesus. In Matthew's gospel Jesus speaks *about* people like you and says that *they* are blessed. In Luke's gospel Jesus speaks *directly to you* and says that *you* are blessed.

As a poor, hungry, or despairing person among others in the crowd, listen closely to Jesus' words and determine if one Gospel version resonates with your mind, heart, and spirit more than the other.

Economic poverty occurs when one lacks currencies such as money and other kinds of wealth.

- What are other forms of poverty in the world and the currencies that define them?

Look at those around you who are "poor in spirit" and name the currencies that they lack.

People "weep" and "mourn" over losses. List literal and figurative losses that make people weep.

- And what besides the death of loved ones, friends, and even strangers do people mourn?

Physical hunger is satisfied with food.

- How does a "hunger and thirst for righteousness" get satisfied?
  – And other hungers?

Look through windows that let you see the poor, hungry, and despairing people throughout the world. Make note of the social, economic, and political forces that allowed them to become poor, hungry, or despairing and keep them entrenched in their poverty, hunger, or place of despair. Name those people, individually and collectively, who provide a word or deed that tells these people they are *blessed*.

Closer to home, look around you at people who live in emotional or spiritual poverty, who hunger for relationship, love, and meaning, and who despair over losses real and imagined.

- What words or deeds would tell them: "You are *blessed*"?

Ask yourself where, when, and how you feel *poor* today.

- What do you lack that makes you poor?
- In your poverty, has there been someone who recognized your physical, emotional, or spiritual poverty?
- If you had enough currency to relieve your poverty, what would you gain?
  – Would you also feel as though something was lost in the process?

Think about that for which you *hunger* today.

- What would it take for that hunger to feel satisfied?

And those times when you have wept:

- What caused the weeping?
- Did anyone show up to comfort you as you wept?

Reach back in time and recall when your body, mind, or spirit felt impoverished. Remember how you hungered for something besides food or wept endlessly. Now know that time in another way. Stand, move around, kneel, or curl up as one who is poor, or hungry, or weeping.

Now take a couple of deep breaths and listen for a voice that says: "Blessed are you."

Again, begin to move, stand, or kneel as one who knows they are blessed.

Take time reflect in your journal.

- Has someone ever *blessed* you when you felt impoverished?
- Who have you called *blessed*?
- Who in the world around you or in your own house—in their poverty, or hunger, or grief —waits to be blessed by your words or actions?
- What poverty, or hunger, or grief in your life still waits for a blessing?
  – Where might it come from?
  – What would it look like?

Mirrors

Loneliness and the feeling of being unwanted is the most terrible poverty.
—Mother Teresa of Calcutta[82]

To have nothing is not poverty.
—Latin proverb[83]

Wherever the poor are heard and respected, the face of God is illuminated.
—Jean-Bertrand Aristide[84]

The capacity to really listen, to put aside our own concerns for the moment, to feel or imagine ourselves in the world of another person and then to communicate our empathic understanding to that person in such a way that he or she feels heard or understood is the foundation for all genuine relationship and solidarity between human beings. This skill is critically important in our relationships to poor people. Their cries must be heard by our hearts.
—John Neafsey[85]

God's politics is never partisan or ideological. But it challenges everything about our politics. God's politics reminds us of the people our politics always neglects—the poor, the vulnerable, the left behind. God's politics challenges narrow national, ethnic, economic, or cultural self-interest, reminding us of a much wider world and the creative human diversity of all those made in the image of the creator. God's politics reminds us of the creation itself, a rich environment in which we are to be good stewards, not mere users, consumers, and exploiters. And God's politics pleads with us to resolve the inevitable conflicts among us, as much as is possible, without the terrible cost and consequences of war. God's politics always reminds us of the ancient prophetic prescription to "choose life, so that you and your children may live," and challenges all the selective moralities that would choose one set of lives and issues over another.

—Jim Wallis[86]

From *Our Mutual Friend*
by Charles Dickens[87]

O Mr. Rokesmith, before you go, if you could but make me poor again! O! Make me poor again, Somebody, I beg and pray, or my heart will break if this goes on! Pa, dear, make me poor again and take me home! I was bad enough there, but I have been so much worse here. Don't give me money, Mr. Boffin, I won't have money. Keep it away from me, and only let me speak to good little Pa, and lay my head upon his shoulder, and tell him all my griefs. Nobody else can understand me, nobody else can comfort me, nobody else knows how unworthy I am, and yet can love me like a little child. I am better with Pa than any one—more innocent, more sorry, more glad!

Who Was That Man?
by Paul Bussan[88]

> I love those movies
> About a stranger
> Who rides into town
> On the back of a horse,
> And proceeds to start
> A chain of events
> That makes each person
> Take stock of their lives,
> So that after he's gone

Everyone's better
Or worse for the wear
Than they were
Before he arrived.

Late Fragment
by Raymond Carver[89]
And did you get what
you wanted from this life, even so?
I did.
And what did you want?
To call myself beloved, to feel myself
beloved on the earth.

From: *Eternal Echoes: Exploring Our Yearning to Belong*
by John O'Donohue[90]

No one else can confer dignity on you; it is something that comes from within. You cannot fake it or acquire it as you would an accent. You can only receive the gift of dignity from your own heart. When you learn to embrace your self with a sense of appreciation and affection, you begin to glimpse the goodness and light that is in you, and gradually you will realize that you are worthy of respect from yourself. When you recognize your limits, but still embrace your life with affection and graciousness, the sense of inner dignity begins to grow. You become freer and less dependent on the affirmations of outer voices and less troubled by the negativity of others. Now you know that no one has the right to tarnish the image that you have of yourself. . . . Even in compromising and demeaning situations, you can still hold your sense of dignity. At such times your sense of dignity will keep a space of tranquility about you. In the Third World, one is often struck by the immense dignity of the poor. Even hunger and oppression cannot rob them of this grace of spirit. If you do not give it away, no event, situation, or person can take your dignity away from you. The different styles of presence reveal how we belong to ourselves.

Easter Morning
by Jim Harrison[91]

On Easter morning all over America
the peasants are frying potatoes in bacon grease.

We're not supposed to have "peasants"
but there are tens of millions of them
frying potatoes on Easter morning,
cheap and delicious with catsup.

If Jesus were here this morning he might
be eating fried potatoes with my friend
who has a '51 Dodge and a '72 Pontiac.
When his kids ask why they don't have
a new car he says, "these cars were new once
and now they are experienced."

He can fix anything and when rich folks
call to get a toilet repaired he pauses
extra hours so that they can further
learn what we're made of.

I told him that in Mexico the poor say
that when there's lightning the rich
think that God is taking their picture.
He laughed.

Like peasants everywhere in the history
of the world ours can't figure out why
they're getting poorer. Their sons join
the army to get work being shot at.

Your ideals are invisible clouds
so try not to suffocate the poor,
the peasants, with your sympathies.
They know that you're staring at them.

ELEVEN

SEEING EVERYTHING

Then [Jesus] entered Jerusalem and went into the temple; and when he had looked around at everything, as it was already late, he went out to Bethany with the twelve. (Mark 11:11)

Reflections
BY CAREN

Fact: The bald eagle's eyesight is 4–6 times sharper than a human's—so sharp that it can see a small rodent almost a mile away. One reason for its extraordinary vision is the eagle's exceptionally large pupils that cause minimal diffraction (scattering) of the incoming light. Another is two *foveae,* or centers, of focus that allow the eagle to see straight ahead and to the side simultaneously. That means these majestic birds can spot a potential meal—such as a dead fish in the water—from several hundred feet above. When it comes to an eagle's focus on fish, bird lovers tell us that this is quite an astonishing feat since fish are darker on top and thus harder to see from above. Of course dead fish tend to flip over onto their lighter side, which signals that dinner is ready. As for small critters that may be a potential meal, they don't stand much of a chance. An eagle flying one thousand feet above open country can overlook three square miles from a fixed position and spot an unsuspecting rodent. Like humans, an eagle sees in color and its eyelids close during sleep.

When I have writer's block, my eyelids rarely close long enough to sleep and surroundings look and feel black and white. And as anyone who has ever had one of these irritating obstructions to creativity knows, they are called "blocks" for a reason. The writer's varieties take many forms and mine not only cause me to stumble but also function like blinders that limit the scope of my imagination and restrict my view of the places I would like to see my story go next. Earlier today, a persistent case of a sputtering and stalled imagination caused me to trip over such a block. So I turned my back on my last written words, moved to the second story window opposite my desk, raised the blinds, and began looking beyond.

We bought this house for the outside more than the inside. All the windows facing west overlook two fairways on a golf course as well as a lake that serves as a repository for mis-hit balls and a haven for fish, turtles, waterfowl, and alligators. Beyond the winding lake that rims the eighth-hole fairway are woods defined by longleaf pine trees producing cones the size of small missiles, bald cypresses with their bony "knees" bulging out of the ground, and live oak dripping with Spanish moss sheltering chiggers, rat snakes, and bats.

When you enter these northeastern Florida woods you must watch for thorny, entangled underbrush, massive webs spun by hungry golden silk or black and gold argiope spiders, and five of the state's six varieties of poisonous snakes. If you're fortunate, when you walk across the Bermuda grass fairways and around the lake and then go to the liminal places where sandy, unpaved cart paths separate the golf course rough from twigs, small bushes, and mulching layers of pine straw bordering the woods, you can often see red fox looking suspiciously at those intruding on their space, wild turkey pecking at the ground, red shoulder and red tail hawks teaching juveniles to fend, a dozen wood storks hanging like ornaments from a tree, whitetail deer leaping to avoid human contact, and an osprey or bald eagle coming in for a landing.

This time, when I look out the window to try to overcome my block and find ways to reframe old ideas or come up with a new one, the bald eagle glides downward and then soars to a treetop eighty or more feet above. Other times I've seen it do this aerial act for thirty minutes or more while waiting patiently for a fish to go belly up, and then skillfully make one final swoop, grab the gold ring, and head for the nest. However, I have yet to discover that nest—the one it must share with its life-long mate. You'd think the nest would be obvious—at least I do. Especially when I'm really looking hard at everything, it shouldn't be that hard to spot a big bowl made of broken branches and twigs that can weigh hundreds and sometimes thousands of pounds. But the nest somewhere in my backyard remains a detail that eludes me—a reminder of just how hard it can be at times to see what is right before my eyes.

Such was the night I decided to get a divorce. I returned home from an afternoon outing with a friend to find my angry husband had totaled the inside of our house. After walking into the midst of my possessions, his possessions, and our possessions scattered everywhere, I slowly began looking at every single thing now torn, broken, and disheveled and at every thing still in its assigned place. I also watched my past, the present, and my future flash like the yellow warning lights in a school zone. And then I focused on details I'd tried so hard to ignore and deny that held me responsible for my role in creating the room around me. What did I say or avoid saying, seeing, doing, or not doing that contributed to a devastating storm trashing the overall picture in my head? Looking around, up, down, and within at everything caused new questions, new angles on old ones, and new perspectives to fill my imagination and spirit with possibilities. Each made my heart pound with a confused mixture of dread and excitement as I acknowledged what I had suspected for years but refused to see—it was already late. As I thrust open the front door and in response it slammed behind me as though it was a broom whisking me across the threshold of a dark chapter of my life, the vague details of a new chapter began to take shape: step-by-step, question-by-question, detail-by-detail carrying me over and beyond every stumbling block in my way.

Wonderings and Wanderings

Throughout Jesus' lifetime, Judea was ruled by the Roman Empire and occupied by Roman armies. The Temple he entered in Jerusalem was the second of two successive sanctuaries in the holy city. Both replaced the portable sanctuary known as the tabernacle that the ancient Hebrews used to contain the Ark of the Covenant during their stay in the wilderness. Within the Temple, the innermost chamber—the Holy of Holies— replaced the tabernacle and contained the Ark. In 586 BCE, the Babylonians destroyed the First Temple, built by King Solomon in 957 BCE, and they exiled the Jews to Babylonia. In 538 BCE the Jews returned from exile and by 516 BCE had rebuilt the Second Temple. Around 20 BCE, approximately eighteen years into the reign of Herod, king of the Jews, the monarch enlarged the building and the surrounding area and lavishly adorned the structure with gold and silver. At the time of Mark's account of Jesus entering the Temple, Pontius Pilate is the Roman prefect (governor). The high priests in the Temple were no longer of priestly descent, but Roman appointees.

The vignette of Jesus going to the Temple takes place immediately after he and his disciples enter the gates of Jerusalem. People greet Jesus by spreading their garments and leafy branches cut from the fields on the road. Those who went before Jesus and the disciples and those who followed cried out words from Psalm 118: "Hosanna! Blessed is he who comes in the name of the Lord." Hosanna is a cry of praise to God that is also translated from the Hebrew as "save, please" or by extension "save now." Jesus then enters the Temple.

Pick a religious, political, national, or financial building or monument that symbolizes and even makes concrete one or more of your most deeply held beliefs and the center of your being. Recall as many reasons as possible why it feels so significant to you. Include not only the positive aspects of what it has stood for, undergone, and survived historically but negative and disappointing ones as well.

Now sit or stand quietly. When you are ready, imagine Jesus' feelings on arriving at an entry gate to Jerusalem after his long journey throughout Galilee. See him finally entering the holy city on a beast of burden. Next, picture him arriving at the Temple and then moving into and through the entryway. The definition of the word *everything* is "all the items, actions, or facts in a given situation." Think about, list, or express with art materials what Jesus sees while looking at "everything."

In your mind or in reality revisit a structure in a major city, your hometown, your house, or your imagination that serves as the definitive symbol of your most deeply held morals and values in the world around you and within. Before entering this space, think about events, hopes, plans, expectations, and dreams that it may embody for you. Look with an eagle's eye around, above, below, beyond, and within you at everything.

After looking around at everything, literally and metaphorically unpack the phrase "as it was already late."

- Is it?

Mirrors

What is meant by light? To gaze with undimmed eyes on all darknesses.
    —Nikos Kazantzakis[92]

> If the doors of perception were cleansed, everything
> would appear to man as it is, infinite.
> For man has closed himself up, till he sees all things thro' narrow
>   chinks of his cavern.
>   —William Blake[93]

A wise man sees as much as he ought, not as much as he can.
     —Michel de Montaigne, from www.thinkexist.com

The Buddha did not enter some new territory: he saw things the way they were. What was extinguished was only the *false view* of self. What had always been illusory was understood as such. Nothing was changed but the perspective of the observer. When asked, "What are you?" by an awestruck would-be follower, the Buddha responded only, "I am awake."
     —Mark Epstein[94]

> Amazing grace how sweet the sound,
> that saved a wretch like me.
> I once was lost, but now I'm found,
> was blind but now I see.
> —John Newton[95]

Capernaum
by Paul Bussan[96]

> You cannot elude your
> destiny, you cannot get
> rid of your talent.
>   —Cardinal Newman

To watch men walk away
When it gets too hard
To get it,

To see women sell out
the best part
of themselves,

To stick
To the self
With passion unheard of,

Is harder than nails.

From *Days of Wine and Roses*, Act III
by J. P. Miller[97]

KIRSTEN: . . . I haven't had a drink in two days.

JOE: Well, that's—-that's terrific.

KIRSTEN: It wasn't easy. But—I wanted to talk to you, so I thought I would try to make myself deserve it, at least a little. Sort of a penance, you might say.

JOE: You'd be surprised how much fun you can have sober, once you get the hang of it.

KIRSTEN: And you've got the hang of it.

JOE: I think so. And believe me, it's the greatest. *She turns away, barely able to keep herself in check.*

KIRSTEN: I want to come home.

JOE, *finally:* It's been a long road, a lot of detours. I can forgive you. I can try to help you, but I don't know if I can take you back. I don't know if I can forget enough. I thought I could, but now I don't know.

KIRSTEN: You're talking about them. Yes, there were plenty of them. But they were nothing. I never looked at them. They had no identity. I never gave anything out of myself to them. I thought they would keep me from being so lonely, but I was just as lonely, because love is the only thing that can keep you from being lonely, and I didn't have that.

JOE: I'm listening, Kirs. *Points left:* There's a little kid in there asleep who sure would like to wake up and find you here, so all you have to do is say the right words.

KIRSTEN: I don't know if I have the right words. That's why it took me so long to get here. You see—the world looks dirty to me when I'm not drinking—like the water in the Hudson when you look too close. I don't think I can ever stop drinking Joe—not completely, like you, I couldn't.

JOE: You could—

KIRSTEN: If I wanted to, really wanted to. But I don't. I know that now. I want things to look prettier than they are. But I could control it if I had you to help me. I know I could. I know I could be all right if we were back together again and things were like they used to be and I wasn't so nervous. But I need to be loved. I get so lonely from not being loved, I can't stand it.

JOE: I want to love you, Kirs, but I'm afraid of you. I'm an alcoholic. I can't take a drink. But I'm afraid of what we do to each other. If you'd only say you'd try—

KIRSTEN: I know this sounds crazy but—I can't face the idea of never having another drink.

JOE: One day at a time. One day at a time.

KIRSTEN, *overlapping:* I can't. I can't.

JOE: Doesn't it impress you at all that I've been sober for almost a year, that I'm delighted to be this way, that I'm working steady and feeling great, that Debbie and I are moving out of this dump into a decent place? And all because I'm sober.

KIRSTEN: You're strong, Joe. That's why I know you can help me now. If we only had it back like it was—

JOE, *too loud:* Back like it—! *He stops himself, remembering Debbie. Then he continues in a low voice:* Do you remember how it really was, Kirs? It was you and me and booze. A threesome. A threesome! Remember? Oh, it was great while it lasted, don't get me wrong—

KIRSTEN, *pathetically eager:* And we can have it back that way! I know we can! If—

JOE: You can't control yourself! You're an alcoholic, same as I am!

KIRSTEN: No!

JOE: You and I were a couple of drunks on a sea of booze in a leaky boat! And it sank! But I've got hold of something to keep me from going under, and I'm not going to let go, not for you, not for anybody. If you want to grab on, grab on, but there's only room for you and me. No threesome. *She turns away abruptly with a kind of desperate anguish, crosses to the "door" and opens it. Then she stops, as though staring out at the world, struggling with herself.*

KIRSTEN, *finally:* I can't get over how dirty everything looks.

JOE: Try it one more day.

KIRSTEN, *turns to face him, hopeless, dead voiced:* Why?

JOE, *motioning left toward Debbie's room:* For her.

KIRSTEN: I'm afraid I'm not that unselfish. You'd give up on me, Joe.

JOE: Not quite yet.

KIRSTEN, *after a moment:* Thanks. Good night. *She turns quickly and starts through the door.*

JOE: Kirs— (*she stops*) Take care of yourself. *She nods, goes quickly through the door and disappears off right. Joe stares after her. For a moment or two it looks as though he is going to call her back. He takes two or three strides towards the door, then stops, holding himself precariously in check. He stands this way for several seconds, rigid, trembling, grimly fighting for the biggest victory of his life. Then, praying:* God—grant me the serenity to accept the things I cannot change. *Lights fade slowly to black.*

Walking Home on an Early Spring Evening
by David Young[98]

> Every microcosm needs its crow,
> something to hang around and comment,
> scavenge,
> alight on highest branches.
>
> Who hasn't seen the gnats,
> the pollen grains that coat the windshield—
> who hasn't heard the tree frogs?

In the long march that takes us all our life,
in and out of sleep, sun up, sun gone,
our aging back and forth, smiling and puzzled,
there come these times: you stop and look,

and fix on something unremarkable,
a parking lot or just a patch of sumac,
but it will flare and resonate

and you'll feel part of it for once,
you'll be a goldfinch hanging on a feeder,
you'll be a river system all in silver
etched on a frosty driveway, you'll

say "Folks, I think I made it this time,
I think this is my song." The crow lifts up,
its feathers shine and whisper,
its round black eye surveys indifferently
the world we've made
and then the one we haven't.

TWELVE

CROSSING THRESHOLDS

[Jesus] said to them, "Strive to enter through the narrow door; for many, I tell you, will try to enter and will not be able." (Luke 13:23–24)

Reflections
BY TED

I didn't know where the thought came from. Although I always seemed to have had some evidence that the elusive memory existed, I could never find or unearth it. But this time the persistent archeologist rummaging in a forgotten storeroom of my mind opened the right door. There, on the other side, the tip of the long-hidden artifact poked through the surface. The sight of it horrified me. I gasped for breath, and as my shoulders slumped I covered my eyes. "Don't you remember you carried the virus that killed Brad?" the archeologist asked. His words pushed me back from the door, and I scribbled a question in my journal: "Do I actually remember the public health nurse telling Mom that I carried the virus that killed Brad?"

My brother Brad and his twin sister, Susan, were born just before my fifth birthday. That summer the nationwide polio epidemic swept children into iron lungs and graves. My mother was concerned about my brother Kirk and me contracting the virus, but not the twins. "Infants are immune to the virus," said our family doctor. "You have nothing to worry about." That belief was obviously flawed, and my short stint in a nursery school to help my mother cope with the new twins, a toddler, and me became the suspected route that polio took to invade our home.

"Do I actually remember the public health nurse telling Mom that I was the carrier of the polio virus that killed Brad?" The quickly jotted words with question marks of all sizes spiraling around them came during a session of the seventeen-day "Study of the Records of Jesus" retreat that I was attending in the mountains of northern California. The leader had just told us: "Find some space in the room. Then take a few moments to imagine yourself as the traveler in the Samaritan story who is beaten, robbed, and left for dead in a ditch by the side of the road." She paused and then said: "Now *be* that Samaritan and lie in that ditch." Although I had already spent five days exploring the life of Jesus of Nazareth, doing exercises that required me to mime Gospel stories, move to music, draw, and work with other art materials, I became aware of an unusual resistance to enacting this parable.

Lying on the cold wooden floor with closed eyes, I looked for images of the Samaritan getting pummeled and left for dead, but couldn't find any. "What's really stopping me from doing this?" I wondered. Then, assuming that we had all entered an altered state of consciousness and become the Samaritan, the leader added, "Each of us have had times in our lives when we felt beaten, robbed, and left beside the road. Remember the first time that happened for you."

As though on cue, I found myself staring at the tip of the lost artifact. "Why this memory now? I can't go there." But the relic continued to surface anyhow: a picture of a five-year-old standing silently in a doorway seeing only his mother's back, his father just behind her, and a woman they called a public health nurse sitting across from them, shaking her head, and saying, "I'm so sorry. . . ."

"That five-year-old Teddy is you," the archeologist said.

"No it's not! You're making it up. You're a goddamn liar!" I yelled back.

Long after others left the session for lunch, I still lay curled up in a fetal position in a puddle of tears. When I finally got up and went to my room to sleep and numb the pain, I impulsively threw on my running shoes and headed for the trail to the top of the mountain instead. As I ran, panic struck as the thirty-seven-year-old memory tripped me and tried to stranglehold me. When I could go no farther, I surrendered, collapsed, and began weeping again.

The urge to pack my things and quietly sneak away overwhelmed me. I still had twelve more days to go and if this was where this retreat was going I wasn't sure I could continue. But going back to North Carolina meant facing a marriage that was ending, my responsibilities as a father to one disabled teenager and to another who was a victim of his brother's accident, and my role as a pastor to a bustling church in major transition. I'd traveled cross-country as a part of a six-month sabbatical and come here to address some unfinished business. But I hadn't imagined this.

Throughout the rest of the day the archeologist continued to open doors and hold up images of other events long ago shelved in that same hidden chamber. *There I am in the hospital in my Daddy's strong hands as he holds me up to look through the doorway at a large, hissing metal tank with hoses and wires that he calls an iron lung. "That's where Brad is," Daddy says as if to comfort me. Fear overwhelms me and then shame follows as I pee in my pants and Daddy says we have to leave.* And then another image: *There's baby Brad in a small wooden "casket," and I don't understand what "dead" means other than I won't ever see Brad again . . . and it makes everyone sad, including me.*

I sat for hours until evening came and, with it, the final session of the day. Standing outside the door to the seminar room, I considered skipping it. Yet something more than curiosity finally pushed me over the threshold.

As those around shared their experiences of miming the Samaritan story, I drifted off, remembering my parents after Brad died. My father was a traveling salesman who also spent many weekends away in the Naval Reserves. "He had an excuse," I reasoned. "But Mom was at home. She was always there to take care of things. Oh my God. Why can't I remember what she looked like? Why can't I remember her face?"

For the next couple of days I pleaded with the archeologist to find an early image of my mother's face after Brad's death, but each door he opened led to dead ends. Frustrated, I commanded him to try harder. "I've lost my mother. I can't see her face. Find it!" When he finally did, I focused on an image of my mother looking at me as a twelve-year-old. I was lying in a hospital bed after a surgeon had removed a cancerous tumor from my leg. "Everything is okay, Ted," she said as she stroked my brow and kissed my cheek.

Back on top of the mountain, where I took a daily retreat from the retreat, I watched the sunset and reviewed all the issues that seemed to connect the dots of my deep-seated behaviors: feeling abandoned, over-achieving, neurotic over-responsibility, and even acting like a know-it-all bully with several therapists of different stripes. "So why didn't you see the obvious? How many times have you repeated the stories of Brad's death and Susan's lame leg in sermons and therapy?" I asked myself. At times, I remembered, I even questioned whether I somehow felt responsible for it all. But only now could I begin to enter that five-year-old's mind—Teddy's mind—and discover the hidden power that the story buried in deep, unearthed recesses of my psyche had over my life.

Polio not only took Brad's life and crippled Susan when it entered our home. It claimed other victims, too. In the moments that I overheard what the public nurse said, in the way that only a five-year-old could hear it, I felt beaten and abandoned and robbed of my mother's attention, love, and compassion. And in a way that only a five-year-old's mind could understand, I hid the painful memory behind a door to a vault that I hoped I would never open again.

Thirty-seven years after Brad's death that archeologist in my mind unearthed a hidden memory. That memory thrust me across a threshold and into questions I had not wanted to encounter; yet, once on the other side it forever changed the landscape of my life. Now, twenty years after going through that doorway, my brothers and sisters and I are faced with literally opening Brad's grave and unearthing what remains of that small wooden casket. It was one of my mother's last wishes that Brad be buried with her and my father. Another threshold to cross. Another doorway to enter.

Wonderings and Wanderings

Jesus says one should "strive" to enter through the narrow door. Describe in your own words what it means "to strive" and to "try."

Locate doorways in your daily life and see those with and without actual doors. Envision familiar ones that you approach, enter, cross from one side to the other and then exit and, perhaps, close behind you. See others that you routinely avoid in your home, workplace, school, shopping centers, homes of friends and relatives, or when traveling. Popular posters titled "The Doors of San Francisco," "The Doors of New York," "The Doors of Cleveland," even "The Doors of Provence" feature rows and columns of local doors. Sit and imagine what a poster of the significant doorways in your life would look like. Or actually create that poster. Use family photos, drawings, and other resources to express doorways that you strove to enter—whether or not you actually passed through.

Recall the feelings and body language that you experience as you approach or intentionally steer clear of some of these doors.

- Where are the narrow doors that you have striven to enter?
- Figuratively, what made them "narrow"?

Jesus said, ". . . for many, I tell you, will try to enter and will not be able."

- When have you tried to go from one place to another in your life and found yourself faced with a narrow door you could not enter?
- Where in your striving did you stop trying? In attempts to get started? When you looked back? Along the way? At the threshold?
- If you strove as far as the threshold but found you could not go one step farther to move beyond it, what real obstacles prevented you?
  - And imagined obstacles such as memories, old audio and video tapes playing in your psyche, and fears?
- Recalling that time, how did it feel to strive, to see, to stand poised, but not risk taking steps to cross the threshold?
- Among those doorways and their thresholds are there ones you felt thrust into and across?
- Striving to enter through the narrow door has its costs. What did you pay for your decision to enter?
- Did you benefit from the *striving* even if you did not enter?

Name a narrow door that beckons you today and asks whether or not you are ready to strive to enter it.

- In the beckoning, what rational thoughts, mixed emotions, and potential disappointments prevent you from moving forward?
- If you are in process, what do you expect will change when you get to the other side?

Mirrors

[T]hat day, for the first time in months, I wasn't fully dominated by either anger or depression. I had crossed some imaginary inner threshold and found a willingness, at least in that moment, to open my heart again. I was willing because I wanted something. . . . I wanted to experience a life that could be that brilliant. Anne Wilson Schaef said, "Choosing not to die is not the same as choosing to live." She's right. Now I found myself no longer satisfied with being half-asleep and half-awake. I wanted to be fully alive.

   —Paula D'Arcy[99]

A threshold is a sacred thing.
   —Porthyrus[100]

After an eternity of seeking, the sudden threshold of seeing and finding
leaves one filled with a strange paradox of ecstasy and grief. I was born
to see.

>   —Joy Page[101]

> "Cheshire Puss," asked Alice. "Would you tell me, please, which
>   way I ought to go from here?"
> "That depends a good deal on where you want to go," said the Cat.
> "I don't much care where," said Alice.
> "Then it doesn't matter which way you go," said the Cat.
>   —Lewis Carroll[102]

Untitled
by Jeláluddín Rúmí[103]

> Drumsound rises on the air,
> its throb, my heart.
> A voice inside the beat
> says, "I know you're tired,
> but come. This is the way."

The God Who Loves You
by Carl Dennis[104]

> It must be troubling for the god who loves you
> To ponder how much happier you'd be today
> Had you been able to glimpse your many futures.
> It must be painful for him to watch you on Friday evenings
> Driving home from the office, content with your week?
> Three fine houses sold to deserving families?
> Knowing as he does exactly what would have happened
> Had you gone to your second choice for college,
> Knowing the roommate you'd have been allotted
> Whose ardent opinions on painting and music
> Would have kindled in you a lifelong passion.
> A life thirty points above the life you're living
> On any scale of satisfaction. And every point
> A thorn in the side of the god who loves you.
> You don't want that, a large-souled man like you
> Who tries to withhold from your wife the day's disappointments
> So she can save her empathy for the children.

And would you want this god to compare your wife
With the woman you were destined to meet on the other campus?
It hurts you to think of him ranking the conversation
You'd have enjoyed over there higher in insight
Than the conversation you're used to.
And think how this loving god would feel
Knowing that the man next in line for your wife
Would have pleased her more than you ever will
Even on your best days, when you really try.
Can you sleep at night believing a god like that
Is pacing his cloudy bedroom, harassed by alternatives
You're spared by ignorance? The difference between what is
And what could have been will remain alive for him
Even after you cease existing, after you catch a chill
Running out in the snow for the morning paper,
Losing eleven years that the god who loves you
Will feel compelled to imagine scene by scene
Unless you come to the rescue by imagining him
No wiser than you are, no god at all, only a friend
No closer than the actual friend you made at college,
The one you haven't written in months. Sit down tonight
And write him about the life you can talk about
With a claim to authority, the life you've witnessed,
Which for all you know is the life you've chosen.

The door
by Miroslav Holub[105]

Go and open the door.
Maybe outside there's
a tree, or a wood,
a garden,
or a magic city.

Go and open the door.
Maybe a dog's rummaging.
Maybe you'll see a face,
or an eye,
or the picture
   of a picture.

Go and open the door.
If there's a fog
it will clear.

Go and open the door.
Even if there's only
the darkness ticking,
even if there's only
the hollow wind,
even if
   nothing
     is there,
go and open the door.

At least
there'll be
a draught.

Entrance
by Virginia Hamilton Adair[106]

We have all known, now and then,
that the place is always there, waiting,
ours for the asking, for the silent stepping out of ourselves
into solace and renewal.

We do not even need a gate,
though it can be pleasantly awesome,
a ritual of entrance.

Some walk straight in,
through the invisible wall of wonder.
Some scramble through a hedge of thorns,
thankful for the pain, the bright drops of blood.
Some enter over the token length of wall;
they like the solid scrape of stone,
the breathless act of climbing.
Once we are in, no matter how,
the secret terrain goes on forever.

When we forget it is there,
then it is gone, and we are left outside
until we remember.

From: Three Darknesses

by Robert Penn Warren[107]

I

There is some logic here to trace, and I
Will try hard to find it. But even as I begin, I
Remember one Sunday morning, festal with springtime, in
The zoo of Rome. In a natural, spacious, grassy area,
A bear, big as a grizzly, erect, indestructible,
Unforgiving as God, as rhythmic as
A pile-driver-right-left, right-left-
Slugged at an iron door. The door,
Heavy, bolted, barred, must have been
The entrance to a dark enclosure, a cave,
Natural or artificial. Minute by minute, near, far,
Wheresoever we wandered, all Sunday morning,
With the air full of colored balloons trying to escape
From children, the ineluctable
Rhythm continues. You think of the
Great paws like iron on iron. Can iron bleed?
Since my idiot childhood the world has been
Trying to tell me something. There is something
Hidden in the dark. The bear
Was trying to enter into the darkness of wisdom.

THIRTEEN

KNOWING ONE'S WILL

They went to a place called Gethsemane; and [Jesus] said to his disciples, "Sit here while I pray." He took with him Peter and James and John, and began to be distressed and agitated. And he said to them, "I am deeply grieved, even to death; remain here, and keep awake." And going a little farther, he threw himself on the ground and prayed that, if it were possible, the hour might pass from him. He said, "Abba, Father, for you all things are possible; remove this cup from me; yet, not what I want, but what you want." (Mark 14:32–36)

Reflection
BY CAREN

To everything there is a season.
And a time for every purpose under heaven.

A time to be born, a time to die
A time to plant, a time to reap
A time to kill, a time to heal
A time to laugh, a time to weep.
—Ecclesiastes 3:1–8

Back in the 1960s, The Byrds recorded a Pete Seeger composition that took a familiar passage from the book of Ecclesiastes and turned it into one of those songs that plays in your head all day long.

The refrain included the phrase "Turn, turn, turn." "Turn where?" I often wonder when the tune spins on my inner turntable. Round and round? Upside down? Inside out? Toward something? Away from something? Into something?

As the nighttime chill in Toledo, Ohio, in 1999 suggested that one season was turning toward another, Ted and I anticipated a fall as spectacular as the promised colors of the century-old trees on our street. In mid-September, my first book was published. And after ten years of turning around an inner-city parish once on the verge of death, Ted was finally seeing the real fruits of his labors begin to ripen.

So the fall of 1999 should have been spectacular. But, as the cliché reminds us, life can turn on a dime, and days after receiving fresh off-the-press copies of my book, a call came. "Pop's back in the hospital," my mother-in-law reported across the miles and hours separating Toledo and the shores of eastern North Carolina. "The doctors are saying he hasn't much more time." A day later, knowing that it could be the last time we might see Pop, Ted and I drove south to visit, talk, and hug him.

Pop was much weaker than he had been two months earlier when Ted and I sat with him and Mom at the Cleveland Clinic and listened to a heart specialist report: "You have a rare condition." The technical medical details that followed turned our churning guts upside down as did the heart-wrenching prognosis: "There is nothing modern medicine can do to cure it or prolong your life." Our reaction must have looked choreographed. Together, four silent bobble heads nodded up and down and swayed from side-to-side while shoulders sagged, hands clutched, and tears welled up in acknowledgment and disbelief.

After months of declining health and questionable diagnoses, we knew from the time his physician sent him to the Clinic that Pop, an acclaimed artist who was a dashing and risk-taking WWII pilot, a renegade from the corporate world, and the father of six, might be entering the final chapter of a storybook life. And even though we were all on the same page, none of us were ready to hear words saying the time to write the epilogue approached.

Pop broke the silence. "If I can't go back to England one last time, I might as well die right now," he declared.

Every summer for more than a decade, Pop and Millie, his beloved wife of fifty-six years, would turn their compass east and travel to England and France. Once abroad, the couple would reconnect with other professional artists who had become some of their dearest friends, and together they would go to the seaside to paint.

"There is one thing I can offer," the doctor said. "It's a drug in a clinical trial. It will not prolong your life. However, it will improve the quality of your life. Enter this trial, begin taking the drug, and you should be able to go to England. You have approximately three months, so make your plans and start packing."

Pop's eyes widened. "I'll do it," he said. "If that means I will go to England it's an answer to my prayers. I have to do it."

Early in September, three weeks after Pop returned from England, Mom's call came to alert us that Pop was in the hospital. Six weeks later, he died enveloped in his family's prayers. Over all those weeks, my book sat on a shelf with an uncracked binding, because life-changing events continued to turn our thoughts, heads, and hearts in many directions. First, a thick, metal swinging door smacked my mother from behind and hurled her across a room. A complicated surgery to repair broken, brittle hip bones followed. "She'll recover completely," the surgeon predicted, not knowing that cross medication was already causing her to suffer a psychotic break. For weeks afterwards, she rambled to no one and everyone—doctors, nurses, therapists, family members, friends, and long distance by phone to me—about pirates holding her hostage on a boat.

I could not be at her bedside in Florida because days before the accident, I discovered a lump in my left breast. First, a needle aspiration in October. No, it isn't a cyst. Next, a sonogram in November. Yes, it is suspicious. Then, a biopsy before Thanksgiving. Yes, it is cancer. I had surgery the first week in December, and as I prepared to begin radiation treatments my mother returned. She was back. Walking, talking about her physical therapy and La La Land journey, and ready to slide back into routines. The only glitch, she announced, was that she needed a pacemaker. "It's practically outpatient these days," she assured me. And so it was, my physician friends said. However, when she went for tests, her surgeon turned into yet another grim reaper. "You have lung cancer," he announced.

Panicked, my mother opted for immediate surgery. "They'll only take one lobe. I'll be fine. Strange that one of our mother/daughter bonds is now cancer," she reflected. The operation, mere months after her hip replacement, took a toll. Bouncing back was difficult but her determination to recover ruled. On the day I finished radiation we made plans for our reunion and victory celebrations. But before I could book my flight, another page turned into a new chapter. My daughter Jamie learned that test reports had, at last, explained some mysterious, ongoing symptoms. "You have multiple sclerosis," the neurologist said.

I delayed telling my mother, who was already praying so hard for herself and me, until I could no longer put it off. Sobbing, she said, "I'm sorry, I'm sorry." Sobbing, I echoed her. She called her rabbi and the next day he knocked on her door. "I don't understand," she said. "I don't understand. But I do know that if God took me right now so that Caren and Jamie would be okay, I would die a very happy person."

Shaking his head, the rabbi replied, "Muriel. You know that God, not us, decides."

"I'm ready to go," my mother said willfully each time we talked. "I keep praying and telling God that I want you and Jamie to have long, full lives and I keep asking Him to take me so that can happen. I wish He'd answer, but I know better."

Days before I was to head south, a late night call came from my sister: "Caren, mom is in the hospital. She had a heart attack."

Feeling like a rag doll with arms being pulled from her sockets, I mumbled, "Jamie's got a doctor's appointment tomorrow. I'll be down as soon as possible."

I got there in time to hold my mother's hand, wrap my arms around her, kiss her cheek, and say goodbye. After the funeral, I returned home feeling fearful. For months now, no one in my family had known why events kept turning as they did or where to turn except to the medical system, each other, and God. What news would come next that would again up-end my life, my family, my world, my heart, psyche, and soul? Would it be my last post-op and radiation check-ups or Jamie's neurology appointment or something unknown?

Everything looks great for the future, my surgeon, my radiologist, and my oncologist each assured me in his and her way the following week. "I'm sorry to hear about your mother," they added. Days later, I went with Jamie for new test results. "So far, every test indicated that you had a progressive form of MS. But these last ones say it definitely is not," the neurologist said smiling. "We're not sure what you have, Jamie, but it's not MS or progressive. We'll find out. You'll be fine. I imagine it must feel like the answer to a prayer."

Wonderings and Wanderings

This chapter of Jesus' story occurs immediately after his Passover dinner with his disciples. It ends with the legendary scene where Jesus' disciple Judas betrays him and he is arrested. Look again at the text and take note of words that paint vivid pictures of Jesus' emotional state and concerns in Gethsemane, a small olive grove outside of Jerusalem. Now ponder the options or alternative actions or plans that might be available to Jesus at this time.

- Assuming Jesus is a choicemaker, what are the choices he faces?
- What might be some of the costs and benefits of those choices?

As Jesus begins to pray, he calls God "Abba," which means "father." Consider all the other names and attributes—positive and negative—that are associated with the word *father*, and explore what the use of this word says to you about Jesus' relationship to God.

Jesus says, "All things are possible."

- What is he affirming about God?

Rewrite in your own words what Jesus asks when he says, "Remove this cup."

- In making that statement, what might Jesus be making known to "Abba"?
- "Not what I want": Why must Jesus express his own will?
- "What you want": Is this an inner struggle or a discernment?
- In your estimation does Jesus already know—and affirm his commitment to—God's will? Or is Jesus trying to discern what God's will could be?
- What more might Jesus know about himself and his relationship to "Abba," as he expresses his will?
- How might Jesus' prayer unfold differences between God's plan and God's will?

Recall how you learned to pray, the times you found yourself praying, and the words you used. Recall the words you use during troubling times.

- What did you—or do you—hope for, want, or expect when voicing those prayers?

Mirrors

The irony of man's condition is that the deepest need is to be free of the anxiety of death and annihilation; but it is life itself which awakens it, and so we must shrink from being fully alive.
    —Ernest Becker[108]

I believe in the sun even when it is not shining. I believe in love even when not feeling it. I believe in God even when he is silent.
    —Inscription in a Cologne cellar, where Jews hid from the Nazis[109]

The creature has nothing else in its power but the free use of its will and its free will hath no other power but that of concurring with, or resisting, the working of God in nature.
—William Law[110]

There is a great difference between defending life and befriending it. Defending life is often about holding on to whatever you have at all cost. Befriending life may be about strengthening and supporting life's movement toward its own wholeness. It may require us to take great risks, to let go, over and over again, until we finally surrender to life's own dream of itself.
—Rachel Naomi Remen[111]

Love Dogs
by Rumi[112]

> One night a man was crying,
> > *Allah! Allah!*
> His lips grew sweet with the praising,
> until a cynic said,
> > "So! I have heard you
> calling out, but have you ever
> gotten any response?"
>
> The man had no answer to that.
> He quit praying and fell into a confused sleep.
>
> He dreamed he saw Khidr, the guide of souls,
> in a thick, green foliage.
> > "Why did you stop praising?"
> "Because I've never heard anything back."
>
> > "This longing
> you express *is* the return message."
>
> The grief you cry out from
> draws you toward union.
>
> Your pure sadness
> that wants help
> is the secret cup.
>
> Listen to the moan of a dog for its master.
> That whining is the connection.

There are love dogs
no one knows the names of.

Give your life
to be one of them.

You Mustn't Show Weakness
by Yehuda Amichai[113]

You mustn't show weakness
and you've got to have a tan.
But sometimes I feel like the thin veils
of Jewish women who faint
at weddings and on Yom Kippur.
You mustn't show weakness
and you've got to make a list
of all the things you can load
in a baby carriage without a baby.
This is the way things stand now:
if I pull out the stopper
after pampering myself in the bath,
I'm afraid that all of Jerusalem, and with it the whole world,
will drain out into the huge darkness.
In the daytime I lay traps for my memories
and at night I work in the Balaam Mills,
turning curse into blessing and blessing into curse.
And don't ever show weakness.
Sometimes I come crashing down inside myself
without anyone noticing. I'm like an ambulance
on two legs, hauling the patient
inside me to Last Aid
with the wailing of cry of a siren,
and people think it's ordinary speech.

Trees
by Howard Nemerov[114]

To be a giant and keep quiet about it,
To stay in one's own place;
To stand for the constant presence of process
And always to seem the same;

To be steady as a rock and always trembling,
Having the hard appearance of death
With the soft, fluent nature of growth,
One's Being deceptively armored,
One's Becoming deceptively vulnerable,
To be so tough, and take the light so well,
Freely providing forbidden knowledge
Of so many things about heaven and earth
For which we should otherwise have no word—
Poems or people are rarely so lovely,
And even when they have great qualities
They tend to tell you rather than exemplify
What they believe themselves to be about,
While from the moving silence of trees,
Whether in storm or calm, in leaf and naked,
Night or day, we draw conclusions of our own,
Sustaining and unnoticed as our breath,
And perilous also—though there has never been
A critical tree—about the nature of things.

The Night is Darkening round Me
by Emily Jane Brontë[115]

The night is darkening round me,
The wild winds coldly blow;
But a tyrant spell has bound me,
And I cannot, cannot go.

The giant trees are bending
Their bare boughs weighed with snow;
The storm is fast descending,
And yet I cannot go.

Clouds beyond clouds above me,
Wastes beyond wastes below;
But nothing drear can move me:
I will not, cannot go.

Denial
by George Herbert[116]

> When my devotions could not pierce
> Thy silent ears,
> Then was my heart broken, as was my verse;
> My breast was full of fears
> And disorder.
>
> My bent thoughts, like a brittle bow,
> Did fly asunder:
> Each took his way; some would to pleasures go,
> Some to the wars and thunder
> Of alarms.
>
> "As good go anywhere," they say,
> "As to benumb
> Both knees and heart, in crying night and day,
> Come, come, my God, O come!
> But no hearing."
>
> O that thou shouldst give dust a tongue
> To cry to thee,
> And then not hear it crying! All day long
> My heart was in my knee,
> But no hearing.
>
> Therefore my soul lay out of sight,
> Untuned, unstrung:
> My feeble spirit, unable to look right,
> Like a nipped blossom, hung
> Discontented.
>
> O cheer and tune my heartless breast,
> Defer no time;
> That so thy favors granting my request,
> They and my mind may chime,
> And mend my rhyme.

FOURTEEN

DENYING TRUTH

Peter said to him, "Even though all become deserters, I will not." Jesus said to him, "Truly I tell you, this day, this very night, before the cock crows twice, you will deny me three times." But he said vehemently, "Even though I must die with you, I will not deny you." And all of them said the same. (Mark 14:29–31)

They took Jesus to the high priest; and all the chief priests, the elders, and the scribes were assembled. Peter had followed him at a distance, right into the courtyard of the high priest; and he was sitting with the guards, warming himself at the fire. (Mark 14:53–54)

While Peter was below in the courtyard, one of the servant-girls of the high priest came by. When she saw Peter warming himself, she stared at him and said, "You also were with Jesus, the man from Nazareth." But he denied it, saying, "I do not know or understand what you are talking about." And he went out into the forecourt. Then the cock crowed. And the servant-girl, on seeing him, began again to say to the bystanders, "This man is one of them." But again he denied it. Then after a little while the bystanders again said to Peter, "Certainly you are one of them; for you are a Galilean." But he began to curse, and he swore an oath, "I do not know this man you are talking about." At that moment the cock crowed for the second time. Then Peter remembered that Jesus had said to him, "Before the cock crows twice, you will deny me three times." And he broke down and wept. (Mark 14:66–72)

Reflections
BY TED

The server handed me a cup of coffee as I pulled up to the drive-through window and in that moment the realization exploded within me: "I'm lying! I'm lying to Dr. Fred. I'm lying to Linda. And I'm lying to myself!"

I had just stormed out of a counseling session with my soon-to-be ex-wife and my therapist. It had gone badly for me. Dr. Fred asked hard questions and I felt backed into a corner. I became defensive and began justifying and rationalizing everything I said. When I couldn't stand the pressure any longer, I announced the session was over and when I reached the door, I slammed it behind me. Getting in the car for a half-hour drive back to my home, I thought coffee would help.

"You're lying," kept ringing in my head as I put the coffee in its holder and stirred in sugar and cream. Driving home, questions flew at me. "If I really believe what I am doing is right, why do I have to lie about it? Why do I feel I have to explain away my actions and words if I believe in myself? What is it that I think I'm lying about anyhow?"

Obviously, storming out of Dr. Fred's office didn't end my therapy session, which just turned into a self-therapy session. Whatever happened back there gripped me and wouldn't let go. I had felt so self-righteous; now I felt raw. As I continued thinking about everything I said to Dr. Fred, I realized I was talking to the wrong person. Those were things I should have been saying to Linda.

I slowly came to see my words were rooted in lies to myself. I was lying about the constant pain I felt after my son Christopher's disabling accident. I was lying to myself by acting strong while feeling impotent. I was lying about the anger I felt toward the reckless driver of the car in which Christopher was riding. I was lying because that driver was a parishioner and I was supposed to be a "forgiving" pastor. I was lying about the sense of loss I was feeling as my marriage began to fall apart. I was lying about being depressed because I had the responsibility of a congregation to care for. I was lying when I told others, "It was just an accident that could have happened to anyone." And maybe that was the biggest lie, because ultimately I couldn't admit how much I felt responsible for the accident that forever changed all our lives. And behind all my lying was my inescapable fear that the "truth" could penetrate my armor and kill me.

On the television series *Grey's Anatomy*, the character Meredith Grey, played by actress Ellen Pompano, once said, "Sometimes reality has a way of sneaking up and biting us in the ass. And when the dam bursts, all you can do is swim. The world of pretend is a cage, not a cocoon. We can only lie to ourselves for so long. We are tired; we are scared, denying it doesn't change the truth. Sooner or later we have to put aside our denial and face the world. Head on, guns blazing. De Nile. It's not just a river in Egypt, it's a freakin' ocean. So how do you keep from drowning in it?"

By the time I pulled off the road and sat looking into a lake, I felt ashamed. Every lie to myself had a counterpart in a lie to someone else. Not just lies to Linda, but to my family and everyone else to whom I was close. Lies that caused others pain and separated me from them and myself.

I drove away feeling roused from a deep sleep. Awakening, I had witnessed a series of self-denials that could not be un-witnessed. "So what do I do now?" I asked over and over. "Am I willing to stay awake and reunite the person I claimed to be, wanted to be, and hoped to be with the one I lost in self-denial? Or will I just cop out and find excuses for going back to sleep?"

"Would you like some coffee before we get started?" Dr. Fred said a week later. I said yes, and as he poured the hot coffee into a cup I reached out, grasped, held onto, and then swallowed my resistance to telling him the truth.

Wonderings and Wanderings

de·ni·al *n*

1. a statement saying that something is not true or not correct
2. a refusal to allow people to have something that they want or that they believe they have a right to
3. an inability or a refusal to admit that something exists
4. a state of mind marked by a refusal or an inability to recognize and deal with a serious, personal problem
5. in a court of law, saying that you did not do something that you are accused of

Recalling other stories in the Gospels, how would you describe the relationship between Jesus and Peter? Name projections—thoughts, feelings, qualities, or impulses—that Peter may unconsciously place on Jesus.

All the disciples swear they will not deny Jesus. Peter does so vehemently and even says, "Even though I must die with you, I will not deny you." The other disciples agree. Yet, when Jesus is arrested and taken to the high priest, Peter is the only one of the twelve who "follows at a distance."

- What compels Peter to shadow Jesus?
  - Is it devotion? Honor? Fear? Duty? Self-interest? Curiosity? Anxiety? Something else?
- Besides the possibility of being arrested like Jesus, what other risks to his body or spirit might Peter face by following Jesus after his arrest?
  - What might be the risks to Peter's psyche or spirit in *not* following Jesus?

As Peter sits among the guards and warms himself by the fire, a servant-girl comments: ""You also were with Jesus, the man from Nazareth." Peter denies the accusation: "And he went out into the forecourt. Then the cock crowed." The cock crowing would indicate the impending dawn.

- What do those images add to your sense of what might be awakening in Peter?

Peter was accused three times of being an associate of Jesus. After the third accusation, "he began to curse, and he swore an oath." Write in your own words what Peter might have said.

- To whom do you imagine the cursing is directed? The servant-girl, the guards, himself, Jesus? Someone else?
- And what about the oath—an oath saying what?

"[T]he cock crowed for the second time. Then Peter remembered. . . . And he broke down and wept."

- In breaking down and weeping, what might Peter now know about himself that he didn't know before?

Look around you at people you see at the mall, the grocery store, in your place of worship, in your workplace, your neighborhood, or even in your family, and wonder about the roles that denial plays in their lives.

- What does it protect them from, cover up, or keep at a distance?

Ask how and when denial has played a role in your life, and reflect on an event, thought, story, or encounter that may have compelled you, forced you, or seduced you into living in denial.

- What did it take for you to stop living in denial?
- In the days or years since then, what has changed?

Ponder the ways in which you might know or discover what you may be in denial about today and what you would do with that denial once you're aware of it.

• Are the costs of agreeing to live truthfully worth the promises?

Mirrors

The worst lies are the lies we tell ourselves. We live in denial of what we do, even what we think. We do this because we're afraid.
—Richard Bach[117]

Loss is the great equalizer that reminds us that we are not omnipotent; it helps us crack open our defensive shell of invulnerability and denial.
—Lama Surya Das[118]

It's not denial. I'm just selective about the reality I accept.
—Bill Watterson II[119]

It is important to examine how we speak. Our words often betray hidden stashes of denial and avoidance. I was comfortable with my euphemisms for death and dying. In the Methodist church my parents took me to as a child, we said "passed away" or "passed over." And in the contemporary pop-healing lingo, we would say that someone made their "transition." Whatever the term, it's just poetic license for the basic fact that human beings die.
—Joseph Sharp[120]

You never know which twist is going to pop that jar open.
—Tim Russert, speaking on the *TODAY* show, quoting his father (February 4, 2008)

Authenticity demands that we allow a place for all our feelings, especially the uncomfortable ones that we'd rather cover over with denial, secrecy, and rigid thinking.
—Joe Perez[121]

From *I Will Not Live An Unlived Life*
by Dawna Markova[122]

Driving away from the cemetery, I decided to do what she never would have dared. I had a little conversation with Death. I explained that I knew I couldn't control how or when it came, but I definitely did not want to die like my mother, with my heart imprisoned behind those walls.

It whispered, "Do you want to die numb?"

"No!" I hissed back. "I'd rather die soft and feeling pain than hard, brittle, and numb. I want to die with my heart free, wide open, wondering and loving fiercely!"

The response was immediate: "Then how do you have to live so you can be sure to die that way?"

My mother's death gave me a better place from which to live. What she loved survived that ugly and undignified ending. It taught me that the will to live and the will to love are intertwined.

I wonder if she knows that I'm now doing what she never could or would. Here, alone in this cabin in the middle of winter, exploring the complexities of interiority, I have found a twisted seed of passion she passed on to me—the seed of denial. Whenever she hurt or was afraid, she turned herself to ice. She left her body, pretended there was no pain or fear. I can see her shrug her thin shoulders now and hear her saying, "If you can't do anything about it, why bother feeling it?"

Up here on this windy mountaintop under this immense white sky, where everything is frozen into dormancy, I am melting my commitment to stay attached to her by ignoring what hurts. Or ignoring despair. Or ignoring fear. If I feel the energy in my body, and don't tell myself any stories about it, if I follow it all the way, drifting down and down until I touch soil where the pain and fear can root, what will it become in the spring? Could that twisted seed of passion, denial, become the full, ripe seed of presence, of coming to my senses, the place where passion abides?

I am letting the ice walls around my heart soften. I am learning not to ignore or abandon myself when I am in pain. In some ways I am orphaned now that the twisted seed isn't an umbilicus. I am an orphan who is also free now to live abandoned and fully alive.

Account
by Czeslaw Milosz[123]

The history of my stupidity would fill many volumes.

Some would be devoted to acting against consciousness,
Like the flight of a moth which, had it known,
Would have tended nevertheless toward the candle's flame.

Others would deal with ways to silence anxiety,
The little whisper which, though it is a warning, is ignored.

I would deal separately with satisfaction and pride,
The time when I was among their adherents
Who strut victoriously, unsuspecting.

But all of them would have one subject, desire,
If only my own—but no, not at all; alas,

I was driven because I wanted to be like others.
I was afraid of what was wild and indecent in me.

The history of my stupidity will not be written.
For one thing, it's late. And the truth is laborious.

From *This Boy's Life*
by Tobias Wolff[124]

When the forms were all in, I sat down to fill them out and ran into a wall. I could see from the questions they asked that to get into one of these schools, let alone win a scholarship, I had to be at least the boy I'd described to my brother and probably something more. Geoffrey was willing to take me at my word; the schools were not. . . .

I was stumped. Whenever I looked at the forms I felt despair. Their whiteness seemed hostile and vast, Saharan. I had nothing to get me across. During the day I composed high-flown circumlocutions, but at night, when it came to writing them down, I balked at their silliness. The forms stayed clean. When my mother pressed me to send them off, I transferred them to my locker at school and told her everything was taken care of. I did not trouble my teachers for praise they could not give me, or bother to have my collections of C's sent out. I was giving up—*being realistic*, as people liked to say, meaning the same thing. Being realistic made me feel bitter. It was a new feeling, and one I didn't like, but I saw no way out.

. . . [Arthur] came up to me in the cafeteria, dropped a manila folder on the table, and walked away without a word. I got up and took the folder to the bathroom and locked myself in a stall. It was all there, everything I had asked for. Fifty sheets of school stationary, several blank transcript forms, and a stack of official envelopes. I slipped them into the folder again and went back to the cafeteria.

Over the next couple of nights I filled out the transcripts and the application forms. Now the application forms came easily; I could afford to be terse and modest in my self-descriptions, knowing how detailed my recommenders were going to be. When these were done I began writing the letters of support. I wrote out rough copies in longhand, then typed up the final versions on official stationary, using different machines in the typing lab at school. . . . Now words came as easily as if someone were breathing them into my ear. I felt full of things that had to be said, full of stifled truth. That was what I thought I was writing—the truth. It was truth known only to me, but I believed in it more than I believed in the facts arrayed against it. I believed that in some sense not factually verifiable I was a straight-A student. In the same way, I believed that I was an Eagle Scout, and a powerful swimmer, and a boy of integrity. These were ideas about myself that I had held on to for dear life. Now I gave them voice.

. . . I wrote without heat or hyperbole, in the words my teachers would have used if they had known me as I knew myself. These were their letters. And on the boy who lived in their letters, the splendid phantom who carried all my hopes, it seemed to me I saw, at last, my own face.

FIFTEEN

UNPACKING WORDS

Our Father, hallowed be your name, Your kingdom come. Give us each day our daily bread. And forgive us our sins, for we ourselves forgive everyone indebted to us. And do not bring us to the time of trial. (Luke 11:2–4)

Reflections
BY CAREN

Instead of asking for daily bread, I made it daily when my children were young. Because taut family finances only stretched so far, I made two batches—the bread we ate together and the other kind that paid off the bills.

In those days I was a single mom and early to rise meant more than getting up before the sun looked like a soft-boiled egg yolk sitting atop a wavering horizon on Lake Erie. It meant mixing flour, yeast, warm water, oil, and other ingredients in time for the composite dough to rest in a covered nest, expand to the right proportions, and enter the oven before other morning rituals commenced. Nagging kids awake. Making sure that faces got washed, teeth looked brushed, breakfast cereal filled but didn't overflow bowls, and that slices of cheap lunch meats were pieced together to cover all corners of thinly sliced remains of yesterday's bread.

On one hand, when things went well, the money saved making bread, yogurt, clothes, and even furniture anew out of others' discards, kept us a few steps ahead of the debt collectors. On the other hand, the "dough" I made working as a freelance writer and music teacher occasionally relieved us of a few old debts I could, at last, pay in full. As for the remaining bills, monetary leftovers at the end of the week served as partial offerings to local debtors who sometimes pardoned the remainders.

In the still of those long-ago nights, hours after the day's juggling act ended, and the kids got their last goodnight kisses, and the words my typewriter typed no longer made sense, and the song I had to rehearse for a student sounded worse than the student's worst effort, I would sit quietly to ponder, then plan, and finally pray. Most nights, my children's bedtime prayers became springboards hurling my monkey mind into recitations on the theme of "Now I lay me down to sleep." While a repeatedly bumbled "*Shema Yisrael . . .*" ("Hear O' Israel, the Lord your God, the Lord is One") owed its origins to not paying enough attention at services in synagogues too long ago attended, other prayers were from recent encounters with spirit-filled words from assorted religious and spiritual traditions. No matter what the original source, each offered hope and some succor at the end of long days filled with scarcity—all except one taught by Jesus and universally called "The Lord's Prayer." *The* one that still felt forbidden twenty years after moving from a Jewish enclave in Brooklyn to New Jersey and being ordered to recite it and not recite it daily in my new high school homeroom.

"It's a Catholic prayer," my father said in his most uncompromising, teeth-gritting tone, "and you cannot say it."

"But I have to. It's a different school and it's the rule. Just like the Pledge of Allegiance," I tried to explain.

"I don't care whose rule it is. You are not going to pray to Jesus," he exploded.

"His name isn't even in the prayer," I mumbled. "What am I supposed to do?"

"You keep your mouth shut or else . . ."

Of course I didn't. The maker of the mandate wasn't in a homeroom where I was one of only two Jews listening to an invisible rule-maker broadcasting, "We will stand to say . . ." over the public address system. To negate defeat on both battlegrounds, I decided to just move my lips with the rest of the students, keep my fingers crossed under my desk, and secretly pray: "Please oh please oh please don't let me get caught." God must have heard and helped me. If my homeroom teachers knew I was merely miming, they never asked me to speak up. And when I told my father I wasn't "saying" the Lord's Prayer, my only penance for that minor fib was to listen to his standing sermon reiterating the fact that Jesus wasn't *our* Lord.

Overcoming the psychic power of that parental sanction took years. Of course, the fact that when I remarried my husband was an Episcopal priest often confounded my process. When I would try to use my voice to pray *that* prayer in his church, only my lips would move. "Just a habit," I'd tell myself. "Of course it's not rational. Yes, you are acting like a fool. You know better." But the cliché about the death of old habits proved true. Attempts to kill off this one were proving the voice in my head still dominated one particular voice in my heart. Until one day, when compulsion caused that voice to pass.

In 1999, my husband's family gathered around my father-in-law's hospital bed to bid farewell to a most beloved man. A rare form of heart disease was exhausting Pop's life, and we knew there were no other medical procedures or miracles to be pulled out of his doctors' bags.

For hours before his six children and their partners arrived, his beloved wife, Millie, had repeatedly wiped the brow, kissed the cheek, and embraced the fragile body of the semi-conscious man whom she married fifty-six years earlier—six weeks after they met. Several times, when his breathing slowed so much it wouldn't float a feather, she expected him to die. But he lingered in a deepening coma instead.

But it now seemed the time for Pop to pass had, at last, come. At first, we tried to make his transition more comfortable by singing "Amazing Grace." But we were a sorry lot that couldn't carry a tune and Pop's sudden agitation suggested we were possibly harming instead of healing. So we stopped and lapsed into silence. Minutes later, God must have yanked my chain. I poked Ted and whispered: "Should you say the Lord's Prayer?" Without so much as a nod he began—just as he had at the bedsides of parishioners. Joining in, we held each other's hands. Millie gently squeezed one of Pop's and someone else his other. And as all of Ted's siblings, their partners, and his mother slowly—ever so slowly—said the familiar words that Pop dearly loved, I found myself praying aloud with them. And with each word's passing, I felt myself hearing the prayer anew. Word-by-word, I found myself embracing a universal meaning not there before. Word-by-word, it seemed like an hour and not seconds passed as we silently hoped Pop could hear us. He must have, because as we collectively sighed, "Ahh-men," he drew his last breath.

Wonderings and Wanderings

Jesus prayed, "Father, hallowed be your name."

- When praying, why might it be important to name the Other?
- As for the word *Father*, what are the positive and negative aspects of this Father's nature?
- What other names or images for this Other are important to you?

"Your kingdom come."

- What might those words tell you or suggest about God's kingdom—then and now?

"Give us each day our daily bread." In your own words, describe the forms and the functions of this daily bread for you.

- Right at this moment, here, now, what is the bread you need the most?
  - Desire the most?

"And forgive us our sins, for we ourselves forgive everyone indebted to us." (In Matthew's Gospel this is translated: "Forgive us our debts as we forgive our debtors.") Describe what you hear in Luke's Gospel when you encounter the word *sin* in your head, or in a Bible, or from a parent, friend, lover, partner, preacher, or rabbi.

- In asking for forgiveness, what are you asking?
- When or how have you known or experienced forgiveness for sins?

Synonyms for *indebted* include: in somebody's debt, obliged, beholden, and owing a favor.

- What are the economic implications of a debt for both parties?
- When have you been—or felt—indebted?

The prayer yokes our sins to our forgiveness of everyone indebted to us.

- How do you understand the relationship between sin and forgiving those indebted to us?

"And do not bring us to the time of trial."

- To what might the word *trial* be referring?
- Is there a time of trial in your life that you now face, fear, or deny?

Once again in Matthew's Gospel, the wording is different: "And do not bring us to the time of trial, but rescue us from the evil one." Those words are also translated as "rescue us from evil." In Greek, the word *trial* can also be translated as *test* or *temptation*.

Ponder a trial that you once endured or one that you are undergoing right now.

- How might the words *test* or *temptation* expand your ability to explain or comprehend the scope of this trial?
- Do you believe that there was an "evil one" or a particular form of evil that was responsible for bringing you into, thrusting you into, or seducing you into this time of trial?

Matthew's prayer includes a petition to be *rescued* from the "evil one" or from "evil." Other ways of saying that include being saved, freed, set free, liberated, salvaged, or let go.

- In your time(s) of trial, what would being rescued look like or feel like?

Rewrite either this prayer, or a version you remember, line by line in your own words. When you're finished, sit with it. When you're ready, in whatever way is comfortable for you, say it or pray it silently or aloud.

Mirrors

Most people do not pray; they only beg.
 —George Bernard Shaw[125]

Words of prayer are repositories of the spirit. It is only after we kindle a light in the words that we are able to behold the riches they contain. It is only after we arrive within a word that we become aware of the riches our own souls contain.
 —Rabbi Abraham Joshua Heschel[126]

When I was a kid I used to pray every night for a new bicycle. Then I realized that the Lord doesn't work that way, so I stole one and asked for forgiveness.
 —Emo Phillips[127]

Prayer does not change God, but changes him who prays.
—Søren Kierkegaard[128]

Our generation is realistic, for we have come to know man as he really is.
After all, man is that being who invented the gas chambers of Auschwitz;
however, he is also that being who entered those gas chambers upright,
with the Lord's Prayer or the Shema Yisrael on his lips.
—Viktor Frankel[129]

Just One God
by Deborah Cummins[130]

(after Wesley McNair)

> And so many of us.
> How can we expect Him
> to keep track of which voice
> goes with what request.
> Words work their way skyward.
> Oh Lord, followed by petition—
> for a cure, the safe landing.
> For what is lost, missing—
> a spouse, a job, the final game.
> Complaint cloaked as need—
> the faster car, porcelain teeth.
> That so many entreaties
> go unanswered
> may say less about our lamentable
> inability to be heard
> than our inherent flawed condition.
>
> Why else, at birth, the first sound
> we make, that full-throttled cry?
> Of want, want, want.
> Of never enough. Desire
> as embedded in us as the ancestral tug
> in my unconscienced dog who takes
> to the woods, nose to the ground, pulled far
> from domesticated hearth, bowl of kibble.
> Left behind, I go about my superior business,
> my daily ritual I could call prayer.

But look, this morning, in my kitchen,
I'm not asking for more of anything.
My husband slices bread,
hums a tune from our past.
Eggs spatter in a skillet.
Wands of lilac I stuck in a glass
by the open window wobble
in a radiant and—dare I say it?—
merciful light.

From *Survival in Auschwitz*
by Primo Levi[131]

And now, oh, so early, the reveille sounds. The entire hut shakes to its foundations, the lights are put on, everyone near me bustles around in a sudden frantic activity. They shake the blankets raising clouds of fetid dust, they dress with feverish hurry, they run outside into the freezing air half-dressed, they rush head-long towards the latrines and washrooms. Some, bestially, urinate while they run to save time, because within five minutes begins the distribution of bread, of bread-Brot-Broid-cheb-pain-lechem-keynér, of the holy grey slab which seems gigantic in your neighbour's hand, and in your own hand so small as to make you cry. It is a daily hallucination to which in the end one becomes accustomed: but at the beginning it is so irresistible that many of us, after long discussions on our own open and constant misfortune and the shameless luck of others, finally exchange our ration, at which the illusion is renewed inverted, leaving everyone discontented and frustrated.

Bread is also our only money: in the few minutes which elapse between its distribution and consumption, the Block resounds with claims, quarrels and scuffles. It is the creditors of yesterday who are claiming payment in the brief moment which the debtor is solvent. After which a relative quiet begins and many take advantage to go to the latrines again to smoke half a cigarette, or to the washrooms to wash themselves properly.

Loaves and Fishes
by David Whyte[132]

> This is not
> the age of information.
> This is *not*
> the age of information.
>
> Forget the news,
> and the radio,
> and the blurred screen.
>
> This is the time
> of loaves
> and fishes.
>
> People are hungry,
> and one good word is bread
> for a thousand.

SIXTEEN

EPILOGUE:
BRINGING FORTH

Jesus said, "If you bring forth what is within you, what you have will save you; what you do not have within you [will] kill you." (Thomas 70)

About The Gospel of Thomas

In the early centuries of Christianity, as a loose confederation of congregations became a more organized institution, various records of Jesus' life, ministry, and teachings gained authority. At the same time, numerous other accounts of those records were dismissed. Eventually the canon of the New Testament became the four gospels of Matthew, Mark, Luke, and John from which we have drawn all but one of the stories and sayings for this book. Today, thanks to archeological findings over the last two centuries, these four gospels are not the only records of Jesus available to us.

In 1945, Egyptian peasants accidentally unearthed several ancient documents (codices) in a pottery storage jar at the foot of a cliff near Nag Hammadi, a town on the Nile River. The story of the discovery of these documents and the circuitous route they traveled before scholars could view them is intriguing, yet it is the content of this library that most fascinates academicians and lay people alike. One of the documents, in what is now named the Nag Hammadi Library, is the Gospel of Thomas.

The Gospel of Thomas is a collection of 114 "sayings" of Jesus. Unlike the biblical books of Matthew, Mark, Luke, and John the Gospel of Thomas contains no narrative of Jesus' life and ministry or accounts of his crucifixion. Although a number of sayings from the Gospel of Thomas have close counterparts in the canonical gospels, many of the sayings simply begin with "Jesus said," without any additional context. Moreover, scholars disagree about the dating of the Gospel of Thomas. Some contend that it was written as early as the middle of the first century, while others date it to the late second century.

So why include a saying from the Gospel of Thomas in Across the Threshold, Into the Questions? Primarily because the Gospel of Thomas offers us an opportunity to explore a record of Jesus' words without preconceived notions and ideas supplied by other "authorities." For almost 2,000 years the Church in its various persuasions has interpreted and reinterpreted the words of the canonical gospels. During most of that time the Gospel of Thomas laid hidden in the sands of Egypt. Since its discovery, scholars, theologians, clergy and lay people have heard, reflected upon, and experienced this record of Jesus with new ears and new eyes and asked questions of themselves and, perhaps, others that may or may not have answers. Upon reading the saying above from the Gospel of Thomas—especially if it is for the first time—you, too, may find yourself wondering about Jesus' words and wandering around and into the implications of the text. As you do so, consider asking this question also: "How might I know this saying to be alive in the world around me and in my own life today?"

Reflections
BY TED

CRAAACK! The four of us went sprawling as the four-inch-thick pole broke. We quickly looked at each other for broken bones or bloody wounds, and then burst out laughing. "I guess that wasn't a good idea," Michael said. "What we need is a bulldozer."

A bulldozer was out of the question and Michael knew it. Using natural materials, we were building a labyrinth in a wilderness area of West Virginia, and the last thing we wanted was to scar the land with machinery. But we seemed to have met our limit with this boulder. At first glance it looked like a stone the size of a small watermelon in the middle of the path. But the more we dug the larger it became.

"I'm not giving up," Scott yelled as he picked up a shovel.

Gary, who kept poking a crowbar into the ground trying to reach beneath the stone stepped back and folded his arms. "This is one big rock. I don't think we can even budge it," he said.

"We'll get this rock out of the ground one way or another," Michael said, as he grabbed the crowbar and angrily thrust it further into the hole Gary started.

"I've got to fix lunch, so I'll leave the three of you to figure it out," I said and started up the hill.

The retreat was going well. Twelve people from four states had joined Caren and me to create a labyrinth in a meadow at our vacation home. The site was bounded by a small stream and carpeted with lush ferns and spongy moss. On the first day, sticks outlined what would become a forty-two-foot labyrinth surrounding a giant black cherry tree. Today—the second day—people dutifully bordered the evolving path with hand-dug stones from the stream bank and filled the winding pathway with wood chips ground from fallen timber. The work was hard, but there was a spiritual underpinning to every effort. Each morning and evening we gathered for readings from sacred and other texts and throughout the day the labyrinth builders reflected on them.

I rang the old school bell to call everyone to lunch, and tired, sweaty bodies dropped tools, chips, and stones to make their way to the deck on the edge of our pond. As we refreshed ourselves with soup, salad, pita and hummus, the talk turned to the "damn" boulder imbedded in the ground.

"Why can't we just leave it where it is, and make the path go around it?" Jody asked.

Scott and Michael both dismissed the idea. "It's just a dumb rock, and I'm not going to be outsmarted by it no matter how deep it's buried. We've got brains and enough brawn. I'm not going home until we get that sucker out," said Michael.

By the time Caren and I had cleaned up, the others had returned to the meadow. Brian and Mark began constructing *inuksuk*, stone cairns that mimic a human form. Their first creation rose out of the ferns as if it were a guardian of the labyrinth. Jody, Diana, and Gerald collected stones and moved woodchips from a nearby pile to the labyrinth. Mary and Nancy picked up fallen branches for the next round of chipping. And while Scott and Michael continued to discuss dislodging the boulder, Gary sat by the stream writing in his journal.

It was late afternoon when the shouts were finally heard, "It's gonna come out! It's coming out!" The commotion drew Gary back. Mark and Gerald dropped their tools and along with Michael and Scott they tugged on the rope that wound through a pulley. Shouts of encouragement went up as they pulled, and the stone finally rolled over the edge of a grave-sized crater.

Jody yelled, "Free at last!" and as Scott and Michael shared a high-five, Gary suddenly exclaimed, "Oh my God," and walked away.

It took a while for Jody and Brian to fill the huge hole with smaller rocks and dirt, and as they did Mark tamped it down with a heavy tree limb. When the ground was level Diana and Phil spread chips on top and soon it looked as though the huge stone had never been there.

Dinner preparations became a boisterous, communal affair as people who had been strangers two days earlier acted like friends. "Say, where's Gary?" someone asked as we gathered to bless fruits of the day along with the grilled chicken, salad, rice and beans, and bread waiting to be devoured. "Who knows where he went? You know how gloomy he tends to be. He'll show up."

In the twilight following dinner we returned to the meadow and found Gary sitting nearby. Four *inuksuk* now stood at the compass points of the labyrinth to protect the sacred path, and as we entered for our winding journey to the huge cherry tree in the center, Gary, in silence, stayed put.

Later as we sat around a fire pit for the evening readings and reflections and to again toast our accomplishments, laughter filled the evening air. "You can't imagine how silly the four of you looked when that pole broke," Diana said as others mimed astonished looks. Suddenly, Gary stood up and started walking away. Michael called after him, "Where are you going Gary? I know you've been in a funk all day, but the fun is just beginning." Gary turned around. There were tears streaming down his cheeks. "I know I've probably been a pain in the ass because I haven't done much today, but this boulder thing really shook me up." We waited for what was next. Gary returned to the circle but remained standing. After a while he finally mumbled, "This is hard to share, but if I don't say something now I think I'll die."

Again everyone watched as the thin, weary, sixty-something man continued to stand in place and stare into the fire while taking sips of his wine. Finally he cleared his throat and spoke to the flames. "I grew up in one of those stereotypical Catholic families. Large, poor, and struggling. My sister is a nun and an uncle and two cousins are priests. The first time I remember being told I would be a priest I was just four years old. By the time I turned fourteen I was sent away from home to enter a seminary."

Stopping to take a deep breath and then sitting down, Gary continued. "I've spent my whole life in the Catholic Church and never doubted it was what I was supposed to do. Then three years ago it all fell apart. I was accused of a crime. It went all the way to trial, and only then did the full truth come out. The accusations were all lies. You'd think that when everyone finally knew for sure that I was innocent that I would have been elated. I was anything but. The accusation and trial destroyed everything. I lost my job, my religious community acted like I was still guilty and shunned me, and most of my so-called friends disappeared. The hardest part was my family saying I had disgraced them and that they were ashamed of me. Only one of my brothers will even return my phone calls."

We sat stunned. I had called Gary after he signed up for the retreat. He lived in another state and had learned about the event from his therapist. All I knew was that he was a clergyman on a long sabbatical. This was the first I had heard anything about this part of his background.

"Today I wanted to help pull that huge boulder out of the ground . . . and I started to help, but then gave up," he said. "When the pole broke it frightened me. It felt violent—like some wild animal inside me was about to spring loose and possibly kill me. I began reliving the feelings of the trial all over again. At lunch, when Jody suggested that we leave the boulder in the ground I silently agreed. And then later, as I sat way off in the distance and watched Scott and Michael struggle to unearth that stone, I all at once saw it as a metaphor for my life. I was deeply embedded in the Church my whole life and never questioned why. But something inside— and I don't know what the hell it is—always made me feel uneasy. Then the accusations came. Like that rock, I was yanked out of the only life I knew. It left this huge hole and ever since I've felt like I've been standing at the edge of a crater looking in."

Sipping wine as if it were a sacrament he continued. "When Scott and Michael finally rolled the stone out of the hole, I saw a truth I resisted my entire life and dared not acknowledge. And for the first time knew it *was* killing me. . . . Maybe it is and it's time I let it. That person doesn't exist anymore."

Gary then looked around at the group for the first time. "After you left I went back to the labyrinth. I was surprised to see the boulder sitting at the entrance—free at last to be something else. For the first time in fifty-two years I am free. I really don't know where I'm going from here, but I know that tomorrow I'm going to wake up, walk down to that damn boulder, touch it reverently, and see where the labyrinth takes me."

Wonderings and Wanderings

Go to a quiet, safe place. Take a candle or an oil lamp with you. Light it and focus on the flame to help you expand your awareness of this passage. Reread the first half of Thomas 70: "Jesus said, 'If you bring forth what is within you, what you have will save you.'" As you ponder what Jesus says, rewrite the passage in your own words.

"If you bring forth what is within you": What does Jesus' use of the word *what* refer to?

- Would you call the "what" that exists "within" your dreams, hopes, desires, passions, and ambitions?
- Or maybe fears, anger, anxieties, obsessions, resentments, questions, and doubts?
- Or. . . .
  - What must you do to become conscious of the "what" that Jesus says "is within"?

Name the reasons you might ignore, deny, and avoid the "what" *that is "within."*

- How do you do that?
- What do you protect by ignoring, denying, or avoiding it?
- What might no longer be safeguarded if *what is within* were to be brought forth?

Think about what it takes to "bring forth what is within you," and what you have to be, or what you have to do, or where you have to go to be—and to do it.

- What saves you? The capacity to bring forth? The content of what is brought forth? Or both?

Now blow out the flame and focus your attention on the wisp of smoke as it disperses into the air. "[W]hat you do not have within you [will] kill you." Name that which is lacking within that can *kill*.

- What must happen to prevent that which we lack within from destroying us?

Jesus says, "[W]hat you do not have within you [will] kill you." Change the word *you* to the words *I* or *me*. Take a hard look at what you do not have within you and determine what you do have to bring forth that will save you.

- What's next?

Mirrors

The very things we wish to avoid, reject, and flee from turn out to be the "prima materia" from which all real growth comes.
          —Andrew Harvey, *Dialogues with a Modern Mystic*[133]

Life is awareness in action. Despite the thousands of hours of old tapes that program our responses, we continue to live because awareness finds new ways to flow. The positive side of awareness—its ability to heal—is always available.
          —Deepak Chopra[134]

You are destined to fly, but that cocoon has to go.
          —Nelle Morton[135]

From *The Soul of the World: A Modern Book of Hours* by *Phil Cousineau*[136]

If the world is, as the poet said, a "vale of soul-making," then perhaps the soul is a vale of world-making. Soul: the blue fire: the fire-roots: the roots of the gods: the gods of the hidden forces: the forces behind the world: the world of soul.

And so the mystery turns. Something strange comes our way, a shadow from the depths, a hint of another dimension, the pulse of the unfathomable. Once nudged, we know we will not sleep until we have found a name for it, a place where we can hear an echo of it, an image for that infernal part of us that is immortal.

Some call it sacred; some, the holy. There, where we wonder with wild hearts, the temple is built, the temple in which we con-template (literally, "make a temple with") the depths. For some, the soul's plunge into the silent hours is deep inside the temple of the earth: for others, an oak grove grown from a scattering of acorns or a stone poem of cathedral where the spirit can rise like incense. And there, where the inner and outer forces meet, is the soul of the world. No one really knows what the soul is, but tremble forth it does, and, just as mysteriously, shudders away again. To paraphrase Gandhi, nothing that we say about it matters, but it's very important that we say it. The question of the soul is precisely this: a questing, a critical movement to research, reimagine, rediscover what it means to live in the depths; to respond to the godless hours, the soulless days, the spiritless years; to recover the sacred. . . .

The soul is the name for the unifying principle, power, or energy that is at the center of our being. To be in touch with soul means going back to the sacred source, the site of life-releasing energy, the activating force of life, the god-grounds; to venture forth and confront the world in all its marvelous and terrifying forces, to make sacred our hours here; to learn to pay such supreme attention to the world that eternity blazes into time with our holy longing. Soul-making, this.

From *Crossing to Avalon: A Woman's Midlife Pilgrimage* by *Jean Shinoda Bolen*[137]

I began to think that the labyrinth in the nave at Chartres can serve as a symbolic map or metaphor for the pilgrimage. Once we enter it, ordinary time and distance are immaterial, we are in the midst of a ritual and a journey where transformation is possible; we do not know how far away or close we are to the center where meaning can be found until we are there; the way back is not obvious and we have no way of knowing as we emerge how or when we will take the experience back into the world until we do. There are no blind ends in a labyrinth, the path often doubles back on itself, the direction toward which we are facing is continually changing, and if we do not turn back or give up we will reach the center to find the rose, the Goddess, the Grail, a symbol representing the sacred feminine. To return to ordinary life, we must again travel the labyrinth to get out, which is also a complex journey for it involves integrating the experience into consciousness, which is what changes us.

From *God Is A Verb* by *David Cooper*[138]

Every particle in our physical universe, every structure and every being, is a shell that contains sparks of holiness. Our task . . . is to release each spark from the shell and raise it up, ultimately to return it to its original state. The way these sparks are raised is through acts of lovingkindness, of being in harmony with the universe, and through higher awareness.

The ramifications of this teaching are enormous. In each moment of existence we have the potential to raise holy sparks. If we are unaware of this ability and are spiritually asleep, then we do not accomplish much, for the medium through which the sparks are raised is consciousness itself.

From *Lost Light*
by Michael Connelly[139]

There is no end of things in the heart.

Somebody once told me that. She said it came from a poem she believed in. She understood it to mean that if you took something to heart, really brought it inside those red velvet folds, then it would always be there for you. No matter what happened, it would be there waiting. She said this could mean a person, a place, a dream. A mission. Anything sacred. She told me that it is all connected in those secret folds. Always. It is all part of the same and will always be there, carrying the same beat as your heart.

I am fifty-two years old and I believe it. At night when I try to sleep but can't, that is when I know it. It is when all the pathways seem to connect and I see the people I have loved and hated and helped and hurt. I see the hands that reach for me. I hear the beat and see and understand what I must do. I know my mission and I know there is no turning away or turning back. And it is in those moments that I know there is no end of things in the heart.

Metamorphosis
by Kevin Anderson[140]

> A pious caterpillar believes.
>
> A pious caterpillar believes,
> an enlightened caterpillar knows.
>
> A pious caterpillar believes.
> An enlightened caterpillar knows
> the winged life.
>
> A pious caterpillar believes.
> An enlightened caterpillar knows
> the winged life
> requires metamorphosis.

Prayer
by Galway Kinnell[141]

> Whatever happens. Whatever
> *what is* is is what
> I want. Only that. But that.

NOTES

1. Elie Wiesel, *Night* (New York: Hill and Wang, 1972), 4–5. Copyright © Elie Wiesel 1972, 1985, © Marion Wiesel [translation] 2006.

2. Annie Dillard, *Teaching A Stone to Talk: Expeditions and Encounters* (New York: HarperPerennial, 1992), 19–20.

3. Chaim Potok, *The Book of Lights* (New York: Ballantine Books, 1981), 323–25.

4. *The Audacity of Hope: Thoughts on Reclaiming the American Dream*, Audible .com recording (New York: Crown, 2006).

5. Frances Klagstrum, *Voices of Wisdom: Jewish Ideals And Ethics For Everyday Living* (New York: Johnathan David Co. Inc. 2001), 6.

6. Herman Melville, *Moby Dick* (Mineola, NY: Courier Dover Publications 2003), 41.

7. From Etheridge Knight, *Letters from Prison* (Pittsburgh: Pittsburgh University Press, 1986).

8. From Charles O. Hartman, *Island* (Boise, ID: Ahsahta Press, 2004).

9. From *Special Orders: Poems* (New York: Alfred A. Knopf, 2008).

10. From Project Gutenberg, a library of 25,000 free ebooks whose copyright has expired in the USA Book listings; public domain.

11. From William S. Cottringer, *Reconciliation*; www.authorsden.com. Used by permission of William Cottringer.

12. From Frederic and Mary Brussat, Spiritualityandpractice.com, accessed June 17, 2008.

13. *Let Your Life Speak* (San Francisco: Jossey Bass, 1999).

14. Sam Keen, *To Love and Be Loved* (New York: Bantam, 1997).

15. John Neafsey, *A Sacred Voice Is Calling* (Maryknoll, NY: Orbis, 2006).

16. *Dhammasaavaka, A Buddhism Primer: An Introduction To Buddhism*, Lulu.com, 2005, 35.

17. Billy Collins, *Picnic Lightning* (Pittsburgh, PA: University of Pittsburgh Press 1998).

18. Grand Rapids: Eerdmans, 2006, 100.

19. *Sunday Times* (London), December 24, 2004, www.timesonline.co.uk/tol/sport/tennis/article1264239.ece.

20. Rainer Maria Rilke, *The Selected Poems of Rainer Maria Rilke*, trans. Robert Bly (New York: HarperCollins 1981), 19.

21. From Linda Pastan, *Carnival Evening: New and Selected Poems 1968–1998* (New York: W. W. Norton, 1998).

22. From Richard Cecil, *Twenty First Century Blues* (Carbondale, IL: Southern Illinois University Press, 2004).

23. Marcus Braybrooke, ed., *Lifelines* (London: Duncan Baird Publishers, 2002), 21.

24. Eddie and Debbie Shapiro, eds., *Voices from the Heart* (New York: Jeremy Tarcher/Putnam, 1998), 119.

25. Samuel Johnson, *The Rambler* (J. Hodges, 1791), 120.

26. John Cook, *Book of Positive Quotations* (Minneapolis, MN: Fairview Press 2007), 515.

27. Starz Special: The Gridiron Gang, (Los Angeles: Eminence Front Productions, U.S. television release September 15, 2006).

28. "Is God Real As A Table?," *Parabola* (New York: Society of Myth and Tradition, February 2007), 50.

29. DVD, directed by James Mangold (2005; Beverly Hills, CA: Twentieth Century Fox, 2006).

30. New York: Riverhead, 2000, 168–69.

31. From Philip Booth, *Lifetimes* (New York: Viking Penguin, 1999).

32. *The Spiritual Life,* quoted in *Four Broadcast Talks* (London: Hodder and Stoughton, 1937), 37.

33. Robert Hass, *The Essential Haiku: Versions of Basho, Buson, and Issa* (New York: The Ecco Press, 1995).

34. Farlex, The Free Library, Aesop.thefreelibrary.com.

35. *Ageless Body, Timeless Mind* (New York: Harmony 1994), 95.

36. John Cook, *The Book of Positive Quotations* (Minneapolis, MN: Fairview Press, 1997), 494 .

37. www.inspirationalquotes4u.com/swedishproverbs/index.html

38. *The Seven Spiritual Gifts of Waiting* (Minneapolis, MN: Augsburg, 2005), 43.

39. New York: Tarcher, 2001, 76.

40. From Kevin Anderson, *Divinity in Disguise: Nested Meditations to Delight the Mind and Awaken the Soul* (Toledo, OH: CLB Press, 2003), 84.

41. From Dorothy Walters, *Marrow of Flame: Poems of the Spiritual Journey* (Prescott, AZ: HOHM Press 2000). Used by permission of the poet.

42. From Ingrid Wendt, *Moving the House* (Rochester, NY: BOA Editions, 1967).

43. *Crossing to Avalon* (San Francisco: HarperOne, 1995), 34.

44. *In the Service of God: Conversations with Teachers of Torah in Jerusalem by Shalom Freedman* (Lanham, MD: Jason Aronson, 1995).

45. Cambridge, MA: Da Capo Press, 2004, 10–11.

46. New York: HarperCollins, 1988, 525–26.

47. From Peter Schmitt, *Country Airport* (Providence, RI: Copper Beech Press, 1989), 13.

48. From a mass-circulated e-mail, with quotes from the Internet.

49. William Ward Adolphous, ed., *The Poetical Works of Alexander Pope* (New York: Macmillan, 1907), 34.

50. *If Prison Walls Could Speak* (Bartlesville, OK: Living Sacrifice Book Co., 1993).

51. "A Woman's Love," in John Greenleaf Whittier, *Songs of Three Centuries* (New York: Houghton, Mifflin and Co. 1890), 302.

52. Jeffrie Murphy and Jean Hampton, *Forgiveness and Mercy* (Cambridge, UK: Cambridge University Press, 1988), 20.

53. Hariette Taylor Treadwell, *Reading-literature* (New York: Row, Peterson, 1918), 77.

54. Robert Turnbull, *Life Pictures From A Pastor's Notebook* (Boston: Harvard, 1857), 4.

55. Benjamin Franklin, *Poor Richard's Almanack, 1758* (Waterloo, IA: USC Publishing Co, 1914), 52.

56. *Star Trek: Deep Space Nine,* Rick Berman and Michael Piller, Season Four 1995 CBS Paramount Television

57. From Coleman Barks, *The Essential Rumi* (Edison, NJ: Castle Books 1995). Used by permission of Coleman Barks.

58. From Michael Counsell, compiler, *2000 Years of Prayer* (Harrisburg, PA: Morehouse Publishing, 2002), 459.

59. *Engaging the Powers: Discernment and Resistance in a World of Domination* (Minneapolis: Augsburg Fortress, 1992), 192.

60. *But I Tell You Jesus* (Newburg, OR: Barclay Press, 2007), 91.61. Internet Movie Database, www.imdb.com/title/tt0067093/quotes, accessed June 4, 2008.

62. London: Routledge, 1992, 182.

63. From: *Eyes Remade for Wonder: A Lawrence Kushner Reader*, (Woodstock, VT: Jewish Lights Press 1998). 133.

64. From Rita Dove, *On the Bus with Rosa Parks* (New York: W. W. Norton, 1999; originally published in *Georgia Review*, Winter 1998).

65. From Nikki Giovanni, *The Selected Poems of Nikki Giovanni* (New York: William Morrow, 1996), 79.

66. Anonymous, Master's Lectures 1923 (Whitefish, MT: Kessinger Publishing, 2003), 56.

67. M. P. Singh, *Quote Unquote: A Handbook of Quotations* (Twin Lakes, WI: Lotus Press, 2007), 25.

68. Mahatma Gandhi, *All Men Are Brothers* (London: Continuum International Publishing, 2005), 59.

69. Yoma 8, 9, in Joseph Telushkin, *The Book of Jewish Values* (New York: Belltower, 2000).

70. New York: Belltower, 2000.

71. From Dionisio Martínez, *Bad Alchemy* (New York: W. W. Norton & Company, Inc., 1995).

72. From Mark Wunderlich, *Ploughshares*, 80, vol. 25/4 (Winter 1999).

73. Caren Goldman, *Healing Words for the Body, Mind and Spirit* (New York: Marlowe & Co., 2001), 76.

74. John Lennon, Paul McCartney, *Help* album, Abbey Road, Capitol Records (US), record, 1965

75. Think Exist, http://thinkexist.com/quotes/with/keyword/first_person/

76. From www.healthjourneys.com, February 13, 2008.

77. Quoted in Garrett Keizer, *Help* (San Francisco: HarperCollins, 2005), 119.

78. From Marge Piercy, *The Art of Blessing the Day* (New York: Alfred Knopf, 1999), 80–81.

79. San Francisco: HarperSanFrancisco, 2005, 142.

80. From Marcia Lee Anderson, "Diagnosis" (Memphis, TN: Stafford Book, n.d.).

81. From David Whyte, *Where Many Rivers Meet* (Langley, WA: Many Rivers Press, 1990), 37.

82. Bill Swainson & Anne H. Soukanov, *Encarta Book of Quotations* (New York: Macmillan, 2000), 923.

83. Creative Proverbs , http://creativeproverbs.com/cgi-bin/sql_search3cp.cgi?boolean=and&field=all&frank=all&keyword=poverty, accessed July 14, 2008.

84. *Eyes of the Heart: Seeking a Path for the Poor in the Age of Globalization* (Monroe, ME: Common Courage Press, 2005).

85. *A Sacred Voice Is Calling: Personal Vocation and Social Conscience* (Maryknoll, NY Orbis, 2006).

86. *God's Politics: Why the Right Gets It Wrong and the Left Doesn't Get It* (San Francisco: HarperSanFrancisco, 2006), 16.

87. United Kingdom: Chapman & Hall, 1869, 259.

88. From Paul Bussan, *A Rage of Intelligence: Poems* (New Haven, CT: PSB Publishing, 2003), 72.

89. From Raymond Carver, *All Of Us: The Collected Poems* (New York: Vintage, 2000).

90. New York: HarperCollins, 1997, 68.

91. From Jim Harrison, *Easter Morning, Saving Daylight* (Port Townsend, WA: Copper Canyon Press, 2007).

92. *The Saviors of God: Spiritual Exercises* (New York: Simon & Schuster, 1960. Appeared in http://www.time.com/time/magazine/article/0,9171,874166-2,00.html.

93. From *The Marriage of Heaven and Hell,* in Robert J. Bertholf and Anne S. Levitt, eds., *William Blake and the Moderns* (New York: SUNY Press, 1983), 165.

94. *The Sun*, Chapel Hill, NC, December 2007, 48.

95. *The Hymnal 1982* (New York: Church Publishing Inc., 1985), #671.

96. From Paul Bussan, *Rage of Intelligence* (New Haven, CT: PSB Publishing, 2003), 2.

97. From J. P. Miller, *Days of Wine and Roses* (New York: Dramatists' Play Service, Inc., 1962), 46–48.

98. From David Young, *Black Lab* (New York: Alfred Knopf, 2006).

99. *When People Grieve* (Danver, MA: The Crossroad Publishing Co, 2005).

100. Stanley Abercrombie, *A Philosophy of INTERIOR DESIGN* (Boulder, CO: Westview Press, 1990), 7.

101. Brainy Quote, http://www.brainyquote.com/quotes/authors/j/joy_page .html, accessed June 11, 2008.

102. *Logical Nonsense: The Works of Lewis Carroll* (New York: G.P. Putnam & Sons 1934), 109.

103. From Jeláluddín Rúmí, *Rumi the Book of Love: Poems of Ecstasy and Longing*, trans. Coleman Barks (San Francisco: HarperSanFrancisco, 2003), 8.

104. From Carl Dennis, *Practical Gods* (New York: Penguin Books, 2001), 72.

105. From Miroslav Holub, *Poems Before and After: Collected English Translations*, trans. Ian Milner (Northumberland, UK: Bloodaxe Books, 1985).

106. From Virgina Hamilton Adair, *Beliefs and Blasphemies: A Collection of Poems* (New York: Random House, 1998), 80.

107. From Robert Penn Warren, *New Selected Poems: 1923–1985* (New York: Random House, 1985), 3.

108. *The Denial of Death* (New York: Simon & Schuster, 1997), 66.

109. Quoted in Zvi Kolitz, *The Tiger Beneath the Skin* (New York: Creative Age Press, 1947), 81.

110. From *Serious Call to a Devout and Holy Life*, quoted in Dorothy Phelps and Elizabeth Howes, *The Choice Is Always Ours* (San Franciso: HarperSanFrancisco, 1989).

111. *Grandfather's Blessings* (New York: Riverhead Books, 2000), 257.

112. From Coleman Barks, trans., *The Essential Rumi* (New Jersey: Castle Books, 1997), 155–56.

113. From Yehuda Amichai, *Selected Poetry of Yehuda Amichai*, ed. and trans. Chana Bloch and Stephen Mitchell (New York: HarperCollins, 1986).

114. From Howard Nemerov, *The Collected Poems of Howard Nemerov* (Chicago: University of Chicago Press, 1981).

115. Emily Jane Brontë, "The Night is Darkening round Me," from The Poetry Foundation archives, http://www.poetryfoundation.org/archive/poem.html?id= 172967, accessed April 19, 2008.

116. George Herbert, "Denial," from The Poetry Foundation archives, http://www.poetryfoundation.org/archive/poem.html?id=181055, accessed January 31, 2008.

117. ThinkExist.com, http://thinkexist.com/quotation/the-worst-lies-are-the-lies-we-tell-ourselves-we/365635.html. Accessed June 3, 2008.

118. *Letting Go of the Person You Used to Be: Lessons on Change, Loss, and*

Spiritual Transformation (New York: Broadway Books, 2003), 13.

119. Calvin & Hobbes wikiquote, http://en.wikiquote.org/wiki/Bill_Watterson, accessed April 17, 2008.

120. *Living Our Dying: A Way to The Sacred In Everyday Life* (New York: Hyperion, 1996).

121. *Soulfully Gay: How Harvard, Sex, Drugs, and Integral Philosophy Drove Me Crazy and Brought Me Back to God,* excerpted on Spirituality and Practice, http://www.spiritualityandpractice.com/books/excerpts.php?id=16955, accessed July 15, 2008.

122. San Francisco: Red Wheel, 2000, 65–66.

123. From Czeslaw Milosz, *The Collected Poems: 1931–1987*, Czeslaw Milosz and Robert Pinsky, trans. (New York: HarperCollins, 1988).

124. New York: Grove Press, 1989, 209, 212–14.

125. *The Sun,* magazine, April 2007, Chapel Hill, NC, 48.

126. *Between God and Man: An Interpretation of Judaism* (New York: Free Press Paperbacks, 1997), 137.

127. *The Sun,* magazine, April 2007, Chapel Hill, NC, 48.

128. *Purity of the Heart Is to Will One Thing* (Radford, VA: Wilder Publications 2008), 17.

129. *Man's Search for Meaning* (Boston: Beacon Press, 1985), 157.

130. From Deborah Cummins, *Counting the Waves* (Cincinnati, OH: Word Press, 2006).

131. New York: Touchstone, 1996, 38–39.

132. From David Whyte, *The House of Belonging* (Langley, WA: Many Rivers Press, 1999), 88.

133. Wheaton, IL: The Theosophical Publishing House, 1994.

134. *Ageless Body, Timeless Mind: The Quantum Alternative to Growing Old* (New York: Harmony Books, 1993), 56.

135. From Susan Witting Albert, *Writing from Life* (New York: G. P. Putnam, 1997).

136. New York: HarperCollins, 1993.

137. San Francisco: HarperSanFrancisco, 1994.

138. New York: Riverhead Books, 1997, 29

139. New York: Time Warner Book Group, 2003, 1.

140. From Kevin Anderson, *Divinity in Disguise: Nested Meditations to Delight the Mind and Awaken the Soul* (Toledo, OH: CLB Press, 2003), 124.

141. From Galway Kinnell, *The Past* (New York: Houghton Mifflin Co., 1985).

FILMS

As mentioned in the section titled Suggestions For Using This Book, below is a sampling of the big screen films and made-for-television mini-series that depict the life of Jesus of Nazareth through a director's vision and a camera's lens. The history of Jesus at the movies dates back to 1898 when a silent screen black and white version of *The Passion Play of Oberammergau* directed by Henry C. Vincent was released. It was followed in 1911 by the French silent film *Jésus de Nazareth* and in 1914 with the production of *The Last Supper* (US). Director D.W. Griffiths included Jesus in scenes in his notorious film *Birth of a Nation* (1915) and a year later in *Intolerance*. The former made its mark in cinematic history for its overt racist views. The latter, considered by many a triumph of the silent era that featured 3,000 extras, looked at the subject of intolerance during four periods of world history. One of those periods (Judean) examines how intolerance led to Jesus' crucifixion. Throughout the last century and into the present one, Jesus has not only been the central "character" in low budget movies and those of epic proportions, he has also made cameo-style appearances or been part of a vignette in numerous ones. For example, *The Robe, Ben Hur, South Park: Bigger, Longer & Uncut, The History of the World (Part 1), Johnny Got His Gun,* and *World Trade Center* include scenes spotlighting Jesus as a vision, in a dream, or merely a shadow.

Color of the Cross (2006)

A biographical motion picture referred to as a *biopic*, this film dramatizes Jesus' life different from films "based on a true story" or "historical films." Biopics attempt to comprehensively tell a person's life story—i.e. Gandhi —or at least the most historically important years of their lives. In this retelling of the 48 hours leading up to and including the crucifixion, Jesus is a black man whose death was the result of a racially motivated hate crime. Rated PG-13.

Godspell (1973)

This G rated big screen version of the successful stage musical is an updated version of the Gospel of Matthew told almost entirely in song. It takes place in New York City in the 1970s where Jesus is a wandering minstrel clown surrounded by his troupe of disciples.

Jesus Christ Superstar (1973)

This version of the rock-opera by Andrew Lloyd Webber and Tim Rice recounts Jesus' life through Judas Iscariot's eyes. A record album led to the stage version which was an international success. The G rated movie was filmed on location in Israel.

Jesus Christ Superstar (2000)

In 1996, a successful new production of *Jesus Christ Superstar* was staged in London. Rather than update the original movie, a home video of the new adaptation of the show was released.

Jesus of Montreal (1989)

This modern-day Passion Play from Canada won top honors at the Cannes Film Festival and 12 genies—Canada's equivalent of the Academy Award. It is a reenactment of the life and death of Jesus by Quebec filmmaker Denys Arcand that takes place in Montreal. As an avant-garde critique of institutionalized Christianity and social ills it becomes a thought-provoking and spiritually challenging retelling of the records of Jesus' life. Rated R.

Jesus of Nazareth (1977)

Because of the controversy surrounding this six-hour made-for-TV miniseries, several sponsors pulled their ads prior to scheduled airings on Palm Sunday and Easter 1977. This depiction of Jesus' life is by Italian director Franco Zeffirelli and it continues to be aired every Easter on the History Channel.

The King of Kings (1927)

In 1923, Cecil B. DeMille's version of *The Ten Commandments* was a box office hit and he hoped to top that four years later with *The King of Kings*. In order to avoid any troublesome publicity while filming, DeMille required his actors to sign legal documents that prohibited them from engaging in "sinful" activity during the filming. It is reported that that "embargo" was most painful for several in the cast. It is a silent film that quotes or paraphrases scripture extensively.

King of Kings (1961)

Acclaimed by the press and popular with theater-goers, this remake of Cecil B. DeMille's original was (and to some extent still is) popular with church groups wanting to view a vintage, cinematic portrayal of Jesus' life. Reissued in 1994 with a PG-13 rating.

Life of Brian (1979)

This religious satire is the story of an infant called Brian who grows up to be regarded as something of a messiah only to find himself in the shadow Jesus, who was born at exactly the same time. Familiar Gospel stories are experienced from Brian's perspective. A British-born parody amply peppered with profanity, it features the irreverent Monty Python cast and an R rating.

Son of Man (2005)

Son of Man, a South African movie and the first to debut at the Sundance Film Festival, takes the story of Jesus and retells it as an African fable. Director Mark Dorford-May sets the scene in contemporary Africa where Jesus is born in a southern town named Judea during a time of civil war and widespread poverty. The question that asks, "What would be happen today, if someone in Africa came forward with the same message as Jesus?" serves as the underpinning.

The Last Temptation of Christ (1988)

This R rated adaptation of Nikos Kazantzakis' novel was also divisive prior to its release. On the one side of the controversy were those who declared it heretical and on the other those who found its portrayal of a doubting Jesus thought-provoking.

The Greatest Story Ever Told (1965)

A favorite of Charlton Heston fans this extravaganza included some of the most spectacular scenes in cinematic history and cameo appearances by a multitude of Hollywood favorites.

The Gospel According to St. Matthew (1964)

The offbeat Italian director and Marxist Pier Paolo Pasolini used a documentary style and amateur cast in this unrated, prizewinning foreign drama that portrays Jesus and his followers as gentle radicals working against the grain of the Roman power structure. Originally titled "Il Vangelo Secondo Matteo," it was released in the U.S. as *The Gospel According to St. Matthew.*

The Passion of the Christ (2004)

Perhaps the most controversial film about Jesus ever made. Unlike other films about Jesus, this is not a panorama of Jesus' life. Instead producer and director Mel Gibson focused his lens on the hours before and during Jesus' crucifixion and in the process created a media blitz unlike any other. Hailed by many as a cinematic triumph and damned by others as anti-Semitic and anti-Jewish, it's definitely a make-up-your-own-mind movie. Rated R.

BIBLIOGRAPHY

Aging with Dignity, Five Wishes, Tallahassee, FL, www.agingwithdignity .org, 1-888-594-7437.

Armstrong, Karen. *A History of God: The 4,000 Year Quest of Judaism, Christianity and Islam.* New York: Ballantine, 1993.

Bond, D. Stephenson. *Living Myth: Personal Meaning as a Way of Life.* Boston: Shambala, 1993.

Borg, Marcus J. *The God We Never Knew: Beyond Dogmatic Religion to a More Authentic Contemporary Faith.* New York: Harper Collins, 1997.

———. *Jesus: Uncovering the Life, Teachings, and Relevance of a Religious Revolutionary.* San Francisco: HarperSanFrancisco, 2006.

———. *Meeting Jesus again for the First Time.* New York: HarperSanFrancisco, 1994.

———. *Reading the Bible again for the First Time: Taking the Bible Seriously but Not Literally.* New York: Harper Collins, 2001.

Chilton, Bruce D. and Jacob Neusner. *Classical Christianity and Rabbinic Judaism: Comparing Theologies.* Grand Rapids, MI: Baker Academic, 2004.

———. *Judaism in the New Testament: Practices and Beliefs.* London: Routledge, 1995.

Crossan, John Dominic. *Jesus: A Revolutionary Biography.* San Francisco: HarperSanFrancisco, 1994.

———. *Who Killed Jesus? Exposing the Roots of Anti-Semitism in the Gospel Story of the Death of Jesus.* New York: Harper Collins, 1998.

Crossan, John Dominic, and Jonathan L. Reed. *Excavating Jesus: Beneath the Stones, Behind the Texts.* New York: Harper Collins, 2001.

Dossey, Larry. *Healing Words: The Power of Prayer and the Practice of Medicine.* San Francisco: HarperSanFrancisco, 1993.

Ehrman, Bart D. *Misquoting Jesus: The Story Behind Who Changed the Bible and Why.* San Francisco: Harper One, 2007.

————. *The New Testament: A Historical Introduction to the Early Christian Writings.* New York: Oxford University Press, 2004.

Friedman, Richard Elliot. *The Hidden Face of God.* New York: Harper Collins, 1995.

Funk, Robert W., Roy W. Hoover, and The Jesus Seminar, trans. and commentary. *The Five Gospels.* San Francisco: HarperOne, 1996.

Herzog II, William R. *Jesus, Justice, and the Reign of God: A Ministry of Liberation.* Louisville: Westminster John Knox Press, 2000.

————. *Parables as Subversive Speech: Jesus as Pedagogue of the Oppressed.* Philadelphia: Westminster John Knox Press, 1994.

————. *Prophet and Teacher: An Introduction to the Historical Jesus.* Louisville: Westminster John Knox Press, 2005.

Hillman, James. *Loose Ends.* Dallas, TX: Spring Publications, 1983.

————. *The Soul's Code: In Search of Character and Calling.* New York: Random House, 1996.

Hollis, James. *The Archetypal Imagination.* College Station, TX: Texas A&M University Press, 2000.

Horsley, Richard. *Jesus and the Spiral of Violence: Popular Jewish Resistance in Roman Palestine.* San Francisco: Harper & Row, 1987.

Horsley, Richard, and James Tracy, eds.*Christmas Unwrapped: Consumerism, Christ, and Culture.* Harrisburg, PA: Trinity Press International, 2001.

Horsley, Richard, and John S. Hanson. *Bandits, Prophets, and Messiahs: Popular Movements at the Time of Jesus.* Minneapolis: Winston Press, 1985.

Howes, Elizabeth Boyden. *Intersection and Beyond.* San Francisco: The Guild for Psychological Studies Publishing House, 1971.

————. *Jesus' Answer to God.* San Francisco: The Guild for Psychological Studies Publishing House, 1984.

Jesus Seminar, The. *The Once and Future Jesus.* Sonoma, CA: Polebridge Press, 2000.

Keen, Sam, and Anne Valley-Fox. *Your Mythic Journey: Finding Meaning in Your Life through Writing and Storytelling.* Los Angeles: Jeremy Tarcher, Inc., 1989.

Kegan, Robert. *In Over Our Heads: The Mental Demands of Modern Life.* Cambridge: Harvard University Press, 1994.

Keizer, Garret. *Help: The Original Human Dilemma.* San Francisco: HarperSanFrancisco, 2004.

King, Karen L. *The Gospel of Mary of Magdala: Jesus and the First Woman Apostle.* Santa Rosa, CA: Polebridge Press, 2003.

Klinghoffer, David. *Why the Jews Rejected Jesus.* New York: Random House, 2005.

Levine, Amy-Jill, *The Misunderstood Jew: The Church and the Scandal of the Jewish Jesus.* San Francisco: HarperSanFrancisco, 2006.

Levine, Amy-Jill, ed. *Women Like This: New Perspectives on Jewish Women in the Greco-Roman World.* Atlanta: Scholars Press, 1991.

Maccoby, Hyman. *Judas Iscariot and the Myth of Jewish Evil.* New York: Free Press, 1992.

Meyer, Marvin. *Judas: The Definitive Collection of Gospels and Legends about the Infamous Apostle of Jesus.* San Francisco: Harper One, 2007.

Miles, Jack. *God: A Biography.* New York: Alfred A. Knopf, 1995.

Moore, Thomas. *Care of the Soul.* New York: HarperCollins, 1992.

———. *Dark Nights of the Soul: A Guide to Finding Your Way through Life's Ordeals.* New York: Gotham Books, 2004.

———. *Original Self: Living with Paradox and Originality.* New York: Harper-Collins, 2000.

Morrison, Mary C. *Approaching the Gospels Together.* Wallingford, PA: Pendle Hill Publications, 1986.

Moyers, Bill. *The Power of Myth: Joseph Campbell with Bill Moyers.* New York: Doubleday, 1988.

Myers, Ched. *Binding the Strong Man: A Political Reading of Mark's Story of Jesus.* Maryknoll, NY: Orbis Books, 1988.

Nelson-Pallmeyer, Jack. *Jesus Against Christianity: Reclaiming the Missing Jesus.* Harrisburg, PA: Trinity Press International, 2001.

Ouaknin, Marc-Alain. *Symbols of Judaism.* New York: Assouline, 2003.

Pagels, Elaine. *Beyond Belief: The Secret Gospel of Thomas.* New York: Random House, 2003.

———. *The Gnostic Gospels.* New York: Vintage Books, 1989.

Palmer, Parker. *The Courage to Teach: Exploring the Inner Landscape of a Teacher's Life.* San Francisco: Jossey-Bass, 1998.

Patterson, Stephen. *The God of Jesus: The Historical Jesus and the Search for Meaning.* Harrisburg, PA: Trinity Press International, 1998.

———. *The Gospel of Thomas and Jesus.* Sonoma, CA: Polebridge Press, 1993.

Phillips, Dorothy, Elizabeth Boyden Howes, and Lucille Nixon. *The Choice Is Always Ours.* San Francisco: Harper & Row, 1975.

Potok, Chaim. *Wanderings.* New York: Fawcett Crest, 1978.

Riches, John. *Jesus and the Transformation of Judaism.* New York: Seabury Press, 1982.

Sanders, E. P. *Jesus and Judaism.* Philadelphia: Fortress Press, 1985.

Sanford, John. *The Kingdom Within: The Inner Meaning of Jesus' Sayings.* San Francisco: HarperSanFrancisco, 1991.

Scott, Bernard Brandon. *Re-Imagine the World: An Introduction to the Parables of Jesus.* Santa Rosa, CA: Polebridge Press, 2001.

Sharman, Henry Burton. *Records of the Life of Jesus (Revised Standard Version).* San Francisco: The Guild for Psychological Studies Publishing House, 1991.

Silver, Abba Hillel. *Where Judaism Differs: An Inquiry into the Distinctiveness of Judaism.* New York: Macmillan Publishing Co., 1989.

Sinetar, Marsha. *Reel Power: Spiritual Growth through Film.* Liguori, MO: Triumph Books, 1993.

Spong, John Shelby. *Jesus for the Non Religious.* San Francisco: HarperSanFrancisco, 2007.

————. *Liberating the Gospels: Reading the Bible with Jewish Eyes.* New York: HarperSanFrancisco, 1996.

Steinberg, Rabbi Milton. *Basic Judaism.* New York: Harcourt Brace & Co., 1975.

Steiner, George. *Real Presences.* Chicago: The University of Chicago Press, 1989.

Telushkin, Rabbi Joseph. *Jewish Literacy: The Most Important Things to Know about the Jewish Religion, Its People, and Its History.* New York: William Morrow, 1991.

Throckmorton Jr., Burton H. *Gospel Parallels: A Comparison of the Synoptic Gospels.* 5th ed. Nashville: Thomas Nelson, Inc., 1992.

Vermes, Geza. *The Changing Faces of Jesus.* New York: Penguin Books, 2000.

Visotzky, Burton L. *Reading the Book: Making the Bible a Timeless Text.* New York: Anchor Books/Doubleday, 1991.

Wink, Walter. *The Bible in Human Transformation: Toward a New Paradigm for Biblical Study.* Philadelphia: Fortress Press, 1973.

————. *Engaging the Powers: Discernment and Resistance in a World of Domination.* Minneapolis: Fortress Press, 1992.

————. *The Human Being: Jesus and the Enigma of the Son of Man.* Minneapolis: Fortress Press, 2002.

————. *Transforming Bible Study: A Leader's Guide.* Nashville: Abingdon Press, 1980.

Documentary and Audio Media (Tapes and CDs)

Mystic Fire: www.mysticfire.com; 800-292-9001

New Dimensions: www.newdimensions.org; 800-925-8273

Public Broadcasting System: www.pbs.org—input "Jesus" in the search engine for a list of online interviews, transcripts, and available media.

Sounds True: www.soundstrue.com; 800-333-9185

Speaking of Faith: www.speakingoffaith.org

The Teaching Company: www.TEACH12.com; 800-832-2412

PERMISSIONS

Adair, Virginia Hamilton, "Entrance", from BELIEFS & BLASPHEMIES, © 1998 by Virginia Hamilton Adair. Used by permission of Random House, Inc.

Amichai, Yehuda, "You Musn't Show Weakness", from Selected Poetry of Yehuda Amichai," © 1996 University of California Press, permission sought from publisher.

Anderson, Kevin, "Metamorphosis" and "Prison", from Divinity In Disguise, © 2003 by Kevin Anderson. Used by permission of Kevin Anderson.

Barks, Coleman, "Love Dogs", from The Essential Rumi, © 1997 by Coleman Barks. Used by permission of Coleman Barks.

Bly, Robert, (trans) "I love the dark hours" by Rainer Maria Rilke, © by Robert Bly. Used by permission of Robert Bly.

Booth, Philip, "First Lesson", from LIFELINES © 1999 by Philip Booth. Used by permission of Viking Penguin, a division of Penguin Group (USA) Inc.

Bussan, Paul, "Who Was That Man?" and "Capernaum" from Rage of Intelligence, © 2003 by Paul Bussan. Used by permission of Paul Bussan.

Carver, Raymond, "Late Fragment", from ALL OF US: THE COLLECTED POEMS. © 1996 by Tess Gallagher. Introduction copyright © by Tess Gallagher Editor's preface, commentary, and notes copyright © by William L. Stull. Used by permission of Alfred A. Knopf, a division of Random House, Inc.

Cecil, Richard, "Internal Exile", from Twenty-First Century Blues, © 2004 by Richard Cecil. Reprinted by permission of the publisher, Southern Illinois University Press.

INDEX